Corporate Growth and Diversification

Corporate Growth
and Diversification

CHARLES H. BERRY

Princeton University Press

Princeton, New Jersey

*Publication of this book has been aided by the Whitney Darrow
Publication Reserve Fund of Princeton University Press.*

Printed in the United States of America
by Princeton University Press, Princeton, New Jersey

Preface

Two views of the large diversified firm, or of the large firm that is diversifying, can be contrasted. On the one hand, the development of large diversified corporations can be, and has been, characterized as part of a trend toward increased corporate concentration generally, with increased market power, increased exploitation of the distortive potential of mass media, with, as an inevitable result, a further increase in the significance of oligopoly structure. The role of diversification in the growth of large firms is attributed not to (socially) efficient patterns of investment activity, but to limitations imposed by antitrust constraints on horizontal and vertical acquisition.

An alternative interpretation would regard such a trend toward increasing diversification by large industrial corporations as one possibly diminishing the significance of precisely those entry barriers which have been most conducive to the development and preservation of market power in oligopoly markets in the first place. If such barriers (other than those deliberately legislated) are typically or even frequently a consequence of the size of the investment required for successful entry, if private (and public) capital markets are organized in such a fashion that the requisite funding for such entry is not readily forthcoming, if the bulk of private domestic investment originates from the retained earnings of large industrial corporations and if those corporations do *not* diversify, these entry barriers will effectively protect large firms in concentrated industries from the competition of small-scale entrants.

If, however, these large firms seek investment opportunities quite independently of their present or past areas of manufacture, the protective potential of entry barriers of this sort will be lessened. In this view—or with this interpretation—the large diversified corporation is regarded as a development offsetting, in part, the failure of equity or capital markets to provide a competitive source of new investment funds in parcels of the necessary size. In the sense that the "multinational" corporation (certainly without unanimous agreement) has been attributed to imperfections in international capital markets (and other restrictions), there is the analogous view of the large diversified firm as the domestic counterpart. In each case, it is not clear that the impact has not been a competitive one within the markets involved.

This book is intended as a first look at this aspect of industrial organization—the growth and diversification of large U.S. manufacturers. It is based in very large part on survey data obtained from the *Plant and Product Directory* published by *Fortune* in 1961 and 1966. These survey data identify the plants, and the 5-digit products of those plants, of the largest U.S. industrial corporations in 1960 and in 1965. When this work was begun, these data were the only publicly available source of records of this sort.

The *Fortune* data are far from perfect. Initially I had hoped to rely on Census data for this work. Because of Census disclosure rules, that was not possible. As a consequence, the measures here reported are a compromise. They are the best estimates the *Fortune* data could generate, but they are approximations. They also fail, because the original *Fortune* surveys were not addressed to such matters, to distinguish diversification and growth by merger from diversification and growth *de novo*. That is a failure of the data. That limitation would not have been present had access to corresponding Census files been possible. Indeed, a major motive for this work was that it might demonstrate how Census establishment data *could* be employed in this kind of analysis without posing problems of disclosure. It remains to be seen just how successful I have been in that regard.

Some of the material and analysis reported here has appeared, though in somewhat different form, elsewhere. Chapter III is the basis of my "Corporate Bigness and Diversification in Manufacturing" (*Ohio State Law Journal*, Vol. 28, No. 3, Summer 1967). Part of Chapter IV appeared as "Corporate Growth and Industrial Diversification" (*Journal of Law and Economics*, Vol. xiv [2], October 1971). The major findings of Chapter V can be found in "Corporate Diversification Between and Among 2-Digit Industry Groups," in *Proceedings: Workshop on the Large Diversified Firm* (Cambridge: Marketing Science Institute, 1973). Chapter VI forms the basis for my "Corporate Diversification and Market Structure" (*Bell Journal of Economics and Management Science*, Spring 1974). The argument of Chapter VII is presented in more detail in "Economic Policy and the Conglomerate Merger" (*St. Johns Law Review*, Vol. 44, Special Edition, Spring 1970). In the meantime I have had the benefit of comments from many readers. Some errors, both numeric and of interpretation, have been corrected. The former, fortunately, have been minor. The latter I hope will still be argued.

This project was begun at the Brookings Institution and completed at Princeton University. It was supported at Brookings under grants from the Alfred P. Sloan

Foundation and from the Ford Foundation. At Princeton, the support of the Woodrow Wilson School of Public and International Affairs is very gratefully acknowledged.

My primary debt is to the advice and encouragement of Joseph A. Pechman, Director of Economic Studies at the Brookings Institution. The basic data processing itself could not have been accomplished without the help, ingenuity, and hard work of George Sadowsky and Joel Rubinstein, then of the Brookings Computation Center. At Princeton, Dennis Smallwood and Stephen Goldfeld, and at Brookings, Roger Noll, read and commented on a variety of aspects of this work, and that helped enormously. So did the careful reading and suggestions of Miriam Brokaw and Sanford Thatcher of Princeton University Press.

William M. Capron, Melinda Varian, Paul W. Mac-Avoy, L. E. Preston, Gisella Erdödy Berry, William G. Shepherd, George Eads, and Allan Zelenitz also contributed importantly to this work at one stage or another. Again I am grateful, but these colleagues share only my thanks, not any responsibility for error of fact, assertion, or analysis.

Finally, the Department of Economics at the University of California, San Diego, provided an ideal setting in which to edit and prepare this manuscript, and a climate, both indoors and out, that could not have been nicer.

Princeton, New Jersey
1974

Contents

Contents

Contents

Corporate Growth and Diversification

I

Introduction

RECENT decades have not been ones during which
the issue of corporate bigness has stimulated much
academic interest or attracted a great deal of popular
political comment. The popular issue has been the behavior and the (needed) social responsibility of major
firms, but not, in general, the legitimacy of their size.[1] It
is not difficult to see why. As Leonard Weiss put it:
"Firms that sell $200 million a year are not small. . . .
Yet a policy of insisting that all firms be as 'small' as they
(viz. Parke-Davis, Hershey, United Shoe Machinery, Sunbeam and McGraw-Hill) would mean breaking General
Motors into 80 pieces and even American Motors into
5."[2] Whether because of the realities of political feasibil-
ity, or because of sheer everyday familiarity, the issue of
corporate bigness *as such* has not been a particularly ex-
citing one.

At the same time, however, the Department of Justice
—the Antitrust Division—and the Courts have come to
employ standards of enforcement and interpretation that
place more emphasis on matters of size alone—size both
of corporations and of markets—than has been charac-

[1] Part of the reason for this reaction *among economists* is undoubtedly the tradition of defining size in terms of relative market shares—and this is true also of the major antitrust statutes,
which tend to be worded in terms of competition and monopoly.
That is not the same thing as corporate size.

[2] Leonard W. Weiss, *Case Studies in American Industry* (New
York: John Wiley & Sons, 1967), pp. 335-336.

3

teristic of such enforcement and interpretation in the past. The law itself has been considerably strengthened, initially by the 1950 amendment of the Clayton Act, and subsequently by several key judicial interpretations. A more recent spurt of merger activity led to the release in July 1968 of guideposts to the structural characteristics of mergers unacceptable to the Department of Justice.[3] Fashionable or not, development of the standards of present-day antitrust has been very much influenced by the growth and position of the nation's major industrial corporations.[4]

Correspondingly, the period has not been one of stagnation or relative decline by large firms. In 1947 the 200 largest manufacturing corporations held 47 percent of the total assets of all corporate manufacturers.[5] By 1968 that share had risen to almost 61 percent.[6] In terms of value added, the 200 largest accounted for 30 percent of all value added in manufacturing in 1947, and for 42 percent—a 40 percent increase—in 1967.[7] It was in large

[3] United States Department of Justice, *Merger Guidelines*, May 30, 1968 (mimeographed).

[4] See, for example, the argument by the Supreme Court in *Brown Shoe Co., Inc. v. United States*: "But we cannot fail to recognize Congress' desire to promote competition through the protection of viable, small, locally owned businesses. Congress appreciated that occasional higher costs and prices might result from the maintenance of fragmented industries and markets. It resolved these competing considerations in favor of decentralization. We must give effect to that decision." 370 U.S. 294, 344 (1962).

[5] Federal Trade Commission, *Economic Report on Corporate Mergers* (Washington: 1969), p. 173.

[6] *Ibid.*

[7] U.S. Senate, Subcommittee on Antitrust and Monopoly, 89th Congress, 2nd Session, *Concentration Ratios in Manufacturing*

part this trend that led the Federal Trade Commission's *Economic Report on Corporate Mergers* to conclude that: "These . . . developments pose a serious threat to America's democratic and social institutions by creating a degree of centralized private decision-making that is incompatible with a free enterprise system. . . ."[8]

That conclusion, however, is not obvious. In an earlier period, Morris Adelman addressed himself to a similar conclusion in the following fashion: "(1) The American economy is highly concentrated. (2) Concentration is highly uneven. (3) The extent of concentration shows no tendency to grow, and it may possibly be declining. Any tendency either way . . . must be at the pace of a glacial drift. What are the implications for public policy? Strictly speaking, none."[9]

Adelman's conclusion was based on a careful consideration of the pitfalls of statistical manipulation in the estimation of corporate industrial structure, and, more important, the belief that about corporate size *per se*— the absolute size of a firm without reference to market position—economics has little or nothing to say.[10]

Industry, 1963 (Washington: 1966), Part I, p. 2; and U.S. Bureau of the Census, *Census of Manufactures, 1967, Special Report Series: Concentration Ratios in Manufacturing*, MC67 (Washington: 1970), Table 1, p. SR2-4.

[8] Federal Trade Commission, *op.cit.*, p. 5.

[9] Morris A. Adelman, "The Measurement of Industrial Concentration," *Review of Economics and Statistics*, Vol. 33, November 1951, p. 295.

[10] For a similar expression of opinion, George J. Stigler, *The Organization of Industry* (Homewood: Richard D. Irwin, 1968), pp. 296-305. See also the statement by Robert Bork in *Task Force Report on Anti-trust Policy* (Washington: May 21, 1960), pp. 1-A to 7-A. Kaysen and Turner have argued: "We would

That is the setting. This book asserts that there is at least one important aspect of recent corporate growth about which economics *should* have something to say— and about which not much *has* been said. The central thesis is that the degree of interdependency of markets contributing to the increased diversification of large corporations is a key (and ignored) element in the interpretation and analysis of large-scale corporate growth. This point, although obvious at a superficial level, has received virtually no general empirical attention, and a good deal of the lip service it has attracted is premised on grounds that are analytically weak if not wrong. The time period at issue is primarily the late 1950's and early-mid 1960's. That is largely dictated by the availability of needed data. Nevertheless, it is a period in the midst of one during which large firms did display more rapid than average growth about which more than a few voices were raised in protest. Chapter II reviews the evidence and the analytics.

Chapter III contains a description of the data on which the empirical sections of this study are based. That description emphasizes the amount of turnover in the

---

discard the general limiting of big business power as an independent goal of antitrust policy. Some change in the size distribution of firms will be a byproduct of the limitation of market power. To the extent that general business power rests on market power, the limitations of one will correspondingly limit the other. Any antitrust policy, if vigorously prosecuted, that goes beyond the regulation of conduct represents (or reflects) some limitation on the general social and political power of big business. An attempt to press the restraint of big business beyond these results . . . would be so costly in terms of other results that we rule it out as a desirable policy." Carl Kaysen and Donald F. Turner, *Antitrust Policy: An Economic and Legal Analysis* (Cambridge: Harvard University Press, 1965), p. 49.

productive facilities of large industrial corporations. Chapters IV and V report the results of an attempt to demonstrate empirically a relationship between corporate growth and increasing diversification. Chapter VI examines the link between changing market structure and increasing diversification by large industrial corporations. The outcome is summarized in Chapter VII.

II

Corporate Size: Concepts and Interpretation

INCREASING corporate concentration of industry poses two problems, one of measurement, the other of interpretation. This chapter is directed to both. Its purpose is to provide a framework for the following chapters. With respect to measurement, even with allowance for substantial error, the data consistently point to relative growth by the largest domestic industrial firms during the past twenty-five years. With respect to the interpretation of that growth, the second section of this chapter illustrates and argues the essential role of market structure to the analysis of this pattern of corporate growth. The following chapter extends that analysis to the question of corporate diversification.

CORPORATE SIZE: MEASUREMENT

What should be straightforward—delineation of the relative size and share of the nation's largest manufacturing (or industrial) firms—is not. The relevance of these measures lies, presumably, in the independence of the interests of different firms. Indeed, the "firm" is typically defined as an independent decision-making entity. But corporations need not be firms in this sense. Many corporations own, or are owned, by other corporations.[1]

[1] Note that such ownership can be far from complete for effective control. Larner, for example, classifies any corporation

8

Other corporations are commonly owned and jointly controlled.[2] The economic entity is the firm. Available records follow the lines of corporate—or worse, in the case of most U.S. Bureau of the Census data, establishment—division.

In those records, the lines of ownership and control are not clear, nor are they easily made clear. For example, and just to illustrate the problem, Federal Trade Commission (FTC) data, reproduced in Table 2-1, show the share of total corporate manufacturing assets reported by the 100 largest and 200 largest manufacturing corporations. The underlying data on total assets for manufacturing corporations are those reported by the *Quarterly Financial Report for Manufacturing Corporations* (fourth quarter) published jointly by the FTC and the Securities Exchange Commission (SEC). Yet in its own report those data are adjusted further by the FTC. In particular, adjustments are made for apparent underestimation of the assets of smaller manufacturing corporations in the

---

among the 200 largest nonfinancial corporations as "immediately controlled by minority stock ownership if *10 percent* or more of its voting stock is held by an individual, family, corporation, or group of business associates" (emphasis added). See Robert J. Larner, "Ownership and Control in the 200 Largest Nonfinancial Corporations, 1929 and 1963," *American Economic Review*, Vol. 56, September 1966, p. 779.

[2] This relationship between independent corporations is, of course, not confined to that of parent-subsidiary. See, for example, Peter C. Dooley, "The Interlocking Directorate," *American Economic Review*, Vol. 59, June 1969, pp. 314-323; *Interlocks in Corporate Management*, a Staff Report to the Antitrust Subcommittee of the House Committee on the Judiciary (Washington: 1965), and also the testimony of John M. Blair in *Economic Concentration*, Hearings Before the Subcommittee on Antitrust Monopoly of the Senate Committee on the Judiciary, 88 Cong. 2nd sess. (1964), Pt. 1, pp. 82-83.

FTC-SEC sample in the earlier years, the omission of some foreign assets in the reporting of the larger corporations to the FTC-SEC, and the inconsistent accounting treatment of advance payments under defense contracting, again in the case of large manufacturers.[3]

The adjustments are not unreasonable, but neither are they entirely reliable. The adjustment for sampling error in the estimation of the assets of smaller manufacturing corporations is based on a comparison between two samples in a single quarter of a single year—the fourth quarter of 1951—and that difference, 9.2 percent, is used to adjust every preceding year's estimate.[4] Foreign assets are added for the largest corporations, not for all corporations.[5] While it is reasonable to suppose that the bulk of foreign subsidiaries of American corporations are the property of the largest manufacturers, evidence to that effect is not available. Furthermore, for the purpose of assessing the changing corporate structure of American manufacturing, it is not immediately obvious that such foreign assets should be included in the first place. The assets of foreign corporations with American subsidiaries —Volkswagen, for example—are not included (although those of International Nickel, a Canadian corporation are. So are the assets of Opel, a German subsidiary of General Motors). Why? That rationale is not clear.

Information regarding advance payments under de-

[3] See Federal Trade Commission, *Economic Report on Corporate Mergers*, Staff Report to the Federal Trade Commission (Government Printing Office, 1969), Appendix B, pp. 716-729.

[4] *Ibid.*, p. 719.

[5] This is not stated explicitly but seems clear from the context. *Ibid.*, pp. 727-728. Such correction of the asset accounts of *all* manufacturing corporations is too big a job—even for the FTC.

fense contracting is not available for years prior to 1951.[6] No adjustment is made in those prior years, and for the later years the adjustment is based only on the accounts of the largest manufacturers. As with the adjustment for unconsolidated foreign assets, the procedure is incomplete.

The data are sensitive to these adjustments. Had none of these adjustments been made, and had the total assets of the 200 largest corporations as reported to the FTC-SEC been compared to the total assets of all manufacturing corporations as published by the FTC-SEC, the resulting relative growth in the share of the 200 largest manufacturing corporations between 1947 and 1968 would have been less than two thirds that shown in Table 2-1.[7] This is illustrated by Table 2-2.

What Table 2-2 suggests, of course, is that the factors for which the FTC adjustment sought to correct tend as a whole to produce an understatement of relative growth by the larger manufacturers. The difficulty is that the adjustments themselves are not totally reliable, and thus the resulting projections of relative growth by the largest manufacturing corporations have to be considered indicators rather than precise measures.

This point can also be pursued on a different basis. Although the data of Tables 2-1 and 2-2 are based on consolidated (domestic) corporate accounts, which the Quarterly Financial Reports assert ". . . eliminates the multiple counting of all interplant and other intercompany trans-

[6] *Ibid.*, p. 728.

[7] This adjustment assumes that the FTC adjustment for unconsolidated foreign assets and inconsistent treatment of advance payments under defense contracting is confined to the 200 largest manufacturers in each year. *Ibid.*, Table B-1, p. 720.

fers . . . and, to the fullest extent possible eliminates the multiple counting of all intercorporate transfers . . . ," this does not mean that *all* such duplication is avoided.[8] Double counting of assets within the manufacturing sector will remain to the extent that the ownership of corporations overlaps without "control" (51 percent ownership), and also to the extent that intercorporate loans are present within the sector. Gardiner C. Means has estimated that in 1962 approximately $10.2 billion of corporate manufacturing assets were in fact unconsolidated investments of some manufacturing corporations in other manufacturing corporations, tending to artificially inflate

TABLE 2-1:

PERCENT OF MANUFACTURING ASSETS HELD BY THE 100 AND
200 LARGEST CORPORATIONS, 1947, 1954, 1958, 1963,
1967, AND 1968

Year	Share of total Manufacturing Assets		Share of Total Corporate Manufacturing Assets	
	100 Largest	200 Largest	100 Largest	200 Largest
1947	37.5	45.0	39.3	47.2
1954	41.9	50.4	43.3	52.1
1958	46.0	55.2	47.1	56.6
1963	45.7	55.5	46.5	56.3
1967	47.6	58.7	48.1	59.3
1968	48.8	60.4	49.3	60.9
Percent Increase, 1947-1968	30.1	34.2	25.4	29.0

Source: Federal Trade Commission, *Economic Report on Corporate Mergers* (Washington: 1969), Table 3.3, p. 173.

[8] Federal Trade Commission-Securities Exchange Commission, *Quarterly Financial Report for Manufacturing Corporations, First Quarter, 1964*, p. 3.

estimates of total corporate manufacturing assets by that amount.[9] In the process, Means further estimated that the 100 largest corporations in manufacturing in that year "controlled" assets of some $6.5 billion in unconsolidated domestic subsidiaries.[10] The effect of these estimates would be to raise the share of the 100 largest manufacturers by about 4 percentage points beyond those shown by the adjusted FTC tabulations. But that again is a rough estimate. Accurate correction is simply not possible.

TABLE 2-2:

PERCENT OF MANUFACTURING ASSETS HELD BY THE 200
LARGEST CORPORATIONS WITHOUT AND WITH PARTIAL
ADJUSTMENT, 1947, 1954, 1958, 1963, 1967, AND 1968

| | FTC Adjusted | | Unadjusted | | Corporate Assets Adjusted Only For: | |
Year	All Assets	Corporate Assets	All Assets	Corporate Assets	Foreign Assets	Sample Change[a]
1947	45.0	47.2	49.5	52.2	51.6	46.8
1954	50.4	52.1	51.0	52.9	53.4	52.4
1958	55.2	56.6	55.0	56.9	56.9	56.3
1963	55.5	56.3	55.2	56.1	56.6	56.1
1967	58.7	59.3	58.8	59.4	59.8	59.4
1968	60.4	60.9	60.4	61.0	61.3	61.0
Percent Increase, 1947-1958	34.2	29.0	22.0	16.9	18.8	30.3

[a] Sample adjustment increased total corporate assets by 9.2 percent in 1947, and by 1.4 percent in 1954. No explanation is given for sample adjustments employed from 1952 to 1955. See Federal Trade Commission, *op.cit.*, p. 719.

Source: Federal Trade Commission, *Economic Report on Corporate Mergers* (Washington: 1969), Table B-1, p. 720, and Table 3-3, p. 173.

[9] *Economic Concentration*, Hearings, Pt. 1, pp. 282-283.
[10] *Ibid.*, p. 282.

13

Similarly, the impact of investment in non-manufacturing activities by manufacturing corporations is hidden in these tabulations. It is probably true that the largest manufacturers are increasingly active in non-manufacturing activities.[11] For example, the total assets of Avco, Inc., one of these large "manufacturers," included, in 1968, the assets of Seaboard Finance, Embassy Pictures, Carte Blanche, and Paul Revere, none of which is a manufacturing concern but each of which was controlled by Avco. As in the case of the acquisition of foreign subsidiaries, it is not clear that the corporate structure of *manufacturing* is rendered more highly concentrated when a large manufacturer invests in this manner in a non-manufacturing subsidiary.

It is also true, and exceedingly important, that these tabulations depend on the classification of the corporations themselves. Is IT&T an industrial corporation? It was so classified in 1968. It was not so classified in 1948. Such a reclassification shifts *all* the corporation's assets to "manufacturing," not just those directly related to manufacturing activity. The FTC tabulations do not indicate the contribution (negative or positive) of this kind of corporate reclassification to relative growth by the 100 or 200 largest. Such an analysis would be interesting, but again is not possible with the limitations of available data.

Census Establishment Data

The purest measures of the structure of manufacturing alone are those of Table 2-3—Census tabulations of value added by manufacturing establishments. *No* foreign establishment is included. *No* establishment primarily en-

---

[11] For a list of large acquisitions outside manufacturing in 1967, 1968, and 1969, see Federal Trade Commission, *Economic Report on Corporate Mergers*, Table 1-13, pp. 677-678.

14

gaged in any non-manufacturing activity is included. *Every* establishment classified by the Census as primarily engaged in manufacturing is included. Relative corporate size is judged, by these data, solely in terms of value added in manufacturing.

TABLE 2-3:

PERCENT OF VALUE ADDED IN MANUFACTURING ACCOUNTED FOR BY THE LARGEST 100 AND 200 MANUFACTURING COMPANIES, 1947, 1954, 1958, 1963, AND 1967

| | Percent of Value Added by Manufacture | |
| | 100 | 200 |
Year	Largest	Largest
1947	23	30
1954	30	37
1958	30	38
1963	33	41
1967	33	42

Source: U.S. Bureau of the Census, *1967 Census of Manufactures, Concentration Ratios in Manufacturing*, Part 1 (MC67(S)-2, 1). August 1970, p. SR2-4.

On that basis, the largest 200 "manufacturing" corporations—not at all the same thing as the largest 200 corporations engaged in manufacturing—accounted in 1967 for 42 percent of all value added in manufacturing. That is the latest Census year for which these data are available. For that same year the FTC estimates the share of total corporate manufacturing *assets* controlled by the 200 largest corporations was 58.7 percent, or approximately 40 percent more. The discrepancy is large. Part of it is undoubtedly to be attributed to the tendency for the largest manufacturers to be more capital intensive than smaller manufacturers—and also less prone to undervalue assets in corporate accounting. However, a sub-

15

stantial part of the difference must also be attributed to the exclusion of foreign and non-manufacturing activity that is explicitly *included* in the usual tabulations of corporate assets.

Both the Census and the FTC-SEC agree, however, that the relative contribution of the 200 largest increased between 1947 and the late 1960's. For the Census data, the increase is from 30 percent to 42 percent of total value added by manufacturing corporations. That is an increase in the relative share of the 200 largest of some 40 percent. During this period, it seems clear that Adelman's "glacial drift" was definitely upward.

CORPORATE SIZE: INTERPRETATION

How, however, is that "drift" to be interpreted? In conventional economic theory, the link between structure and (predicted) performance is simplistic and well known. The smaller the firm *within its market*, the less likely that any action taken by that firm will be significant or measurable within that market, and the more likely that such a firm will act both independently of others and with the assumption that market parameters (e.g., price) will be unaffected.[12] Where, however, the firm is large within its market, action by the firm will no longer be insignificant in terms of the market as a whole, and hence the response of that market becomes an input to the decision-making process of the firm in question. Where a few such firms dominate a market, the implication is

---

[12] One of the clearest statements of this is Scitovsky's. See Tibor Scitovsky, "Economic Theory and the Measurement of Concentration," in National Bureau of Economic Research, *Business Concentration and Price Policy* (Princeton: Princeton University Press, 1955), pp. 101-118.

that joint, rather than independent, courses of action will have substantial appeal, and that competition among the few will be imperfect at best. This is the basis of most measures of market structure. The concentration ratio is the most familiar, and a substantial body of empirical evidence supports the relevance of that measure to the analysis of market performance.[13]

Market structure, however, is not at all the same thing as the *corporate* structure of industry. The concentration of a particular market is to be judged by the relative size of the largest sellers within that market, by the concentration of sales, not by any measure of the relative, or absolute, size of the firms that are the largest sellers. The size of a particular firm—*in toto*, counting *all* its sales or assets—is irrelevant to the determination of the relative contribution of its sales within a particular market. The corporate structure of industry—measures of the relative size of *firms*—can change quite independently of the structure of markets. Indeed, this appears to have been generally true during most of the twenty-odd-year period for which measures of the corporate structure of industry are reported above.[14] The interesting question is what

[13] For some examples of interesting work along these lines, see Norman R. Collins and Lee E. Preston, *Concentration and Price-Cost Margins in Manufacturing* (Berkeley: University of California Press, 1968); Leonard W. Weiss, "Average Concentration Ratios and Economic Performance," *Journal of Industrial Economics*, Vol. II, No. 3, July 1963, pp. 237-253; William S. Comanor and Thomas A. Wilson, "Advertising, Market Structure and Performance," *Review of Economics and Statistics*, Vol. 49, November 1967, pp. 423-440.

[14] It is not easy to summarize accurately change in the structure of the individual 4-digit manufacturing industries during this period. Study Paper Number 2 of the *Studies by the Staff of the Cabinet Committee on Price Stability* describes the pattern

consideration of corporate size adds to the significance of market structure in the analysis of industry performance.

Corporate Bigness as a Source of Monopoly Power

Starting with Corwin Edwards, any number of writers have painstakingly itemized the competitive options open

---

as follows: "Average market concentration of manufacturing industries has shown no marked tendency to increase or decrease between 1947 and 1966, according to an analysis of 213 essentially comparable industries. The average level of 4-firm concentration for all industries was 41.2 percent in 1947 and 41.8 percent in 1966. In 78 industries, 4-firm concentration ratios declined by 3 percentage points or more and in 88 industries concentration increased by 3 percentage points or more." See *Studies by the Staff of the Cabinet Committee on Price Stability* (Washington: January 1969), p. 58.

The study paper, however, goes on to note first that average 8-firm concentration ratios show a slightly higher rate of increase, and, second, that, for consumer goods industries, average 4-firm concentration rose from 34.8 percent to 39.6 percent, while in producer goods industries it declined 45.1 percent to 43.4 percent. All these averages are, however, unweighted; and weighting by industry size results in a higher overall increase. Scherer, for example, shows this (though for a different sample of industries) in the case of value added weights, but concludes: "All in all, the patterns revealed are sufficiently complex and varied to mask evidence of an unambiguous long-term general trend. We are led to conclude that if market concentration is increasing in the manufacturing sector, it is not doing so in a spectacular, consistent fashion." See F. M. Scherer, *Industrial Market Structure and Economic Performance* (Chicago: Rand McNally, 1970), p. 63. See also William G. Shepherd, "Trends of Concentration in American Manufacturing Industries," *Review of Economics and Statistics*, Vol. 46, May 1964, pp. 200-212, and below, Chapter VI, pp. 124 to 125, for some additional discussion of the underlying data.

to the firm whose sales in a particular market are only a fraction of its sales in all markets.[15] The list is long. It is also superficially appealing.

The welfare of the multi-product firm obviously does not vary solely with its success in any particular market. The firm *could* incur substantial losses in any given market without incurring any necessary loss over all. Cross-subsidization is obviously an option available to the multi-product firm that is not an option to the single-product firm, provided that firms must continuously avoid a net loss position.[16]

Similarly, the firm that has power in one market *may* choose to exploit that power in related markets to the detriment of the firm's competitors in those markets. Exclusive dealing, reciprocal dealing, and tie-in selling are frequently cited as illustrations of the exercise of this form of leverage by the multi-product and hence (by assumption) larger firm.[17]

[15] See Corwin D. Edwards, "Conglomerate Bigness as a Source of Power," in National Bureau of Economic Research, *Business Concentration and Price Policy* (Princeton: Princeton University Press, 1955), pp. 331-359. See also Federal Trade Commission, "Conglomerate Power—Sources and Consequences," in *Economic Report on Corporate Mergers* (Washington: 1969), pp. 321-471.

[16] Cross-subsidization is generally defined as the use of earnings from one activity to finance losses in another. *Ibid.*, p. 398.

[17] Exclusive dealing is the practice, by a manufacturer, of selling only to buyers (typically distributors) who deal exclusively in the products of that manufacturer. Reciprocal dealing results when two manufacturers agree to buy one from another. Tie-in selling (or a tying contract) is present when a manufacturer makes available a given product *only* if the buyer agrees to use other (related) products of that manufacturer in conjunction with that first product. For example, the requirement that a retailer of an automobile manufacturer's cars and trucks

Leverage and Cross-Subsidization

But analysis of that "leverage" is far less straightforward than the demonstration that such leverage is possible. For example, the consequences of structural imperfection within markets are typically argued to be that product prices and/or corporate earnings will tend, in such markets, to be above competitive levels. Under oligopoly, price rigidity, combined with the presence of costly non-price competitive activity, is often suggested. In either case, the implication is that prices will be higher than optimal.[18]

But the implication of "cross-subsidization" by the multi-product firm suggests the opposite—that such a firm may *under*-price rather than over-price.[19] Now it is perfectly true that those who argue the ill effects of cross-subsidization see it as a device through which the large multi-product firm can obtain control of such markets, at which point it is assumed that prices will rise to and above

---

not retail other makes of cars and trucks would be exclusive dealing by that manufacturer. The requirement that the dealer use only "original" replacement parts, supplied by the manufacturer in any repairs undertaken, would be a tying contract. Agreement by the automobile manufacturer to equip all new cars and trucks with the tires of a given manufacturer of tires on condition that the latter corporation's company cars are the product of the former, would be reciprocal dealing.

[18] Oligopoly theories are diverse, but this is surely a conclusion common to most, if not all. For a recent attempt to summarize the literature in this area, see F. M. Scherer, *op.cit.*, pp. 131-182.

[19] The resource allocative implications of under-pricing are, of course, equally adverse. As is indicated below, however, the cross-subsidization argument normally implies that such under-pricing is only temporary.

competitive levels.[20] It can be asserted that the evidence supporting such a pattern of dynamic behavior is largely speculative, but that is not the point. The point is that any advantage to the firm of cross-subsidization occurs only when a position of dominance *within* the market is achieved. And that reduces cross-subsidization to a vague and largely untestable dynamic explanation of the development of market power that neither adds nor detracts from the generally anticipated consequences of market power when it does exist.

Two further aspects should be noted. First, the "theory," insofar as it can be called that, is a theory of behavior applicable to any multi-product firm. It does not apply specifically to the large firm, unless it is argued that only the large firm is in a position to anticipate market control. In that case the theory relates only to the financial resources available to the firm, and has nothing to do with market position or power in any other industry.

Second, if market control is not achieved, or if it is dealt with effectively when it arises regardless of its origin, cross-subsidization is not an attractive alternative to the firm unless it seeks growth at the expense of earnings. Such behavior can be argued to follow from the separation of ownership and control in the large widely held

[20] This is a familiar charge in antitrust litigation. See, for example, Robert C. Brooks, Jr., "Injury to Competition Under the Robinson Patman Act," *University of Pennsylvania Law Review*, Vol. 109, April 1961, pp. 777-832. See also, however, *Task Force Report on Antitrust Policy* (Washington: May 21, 1969), pp. IV-1 to IV-10. For an outstanding analysis of this alleged practice in action, see M. A. Adelman, *A & P: A Study in Price-Cost Behavior and Public Policy* (Cambridge: Harvard University Press, 1959).

corporation.[21] Again, however, cross-subsidization is not needed for such behavior, and the consequences are opposite to those generally assumed to follow from the possession of market power or the presence of structural imperfection within markets.

Tying Contracts

Tie-in selling and exclusive dealing—two other traditional illustrations of leverage—are more interesting, but once more have little to do with *corporate* size or concentration. Each has meaning only where markets are interrelated and (in the absence of externally controlled prices) where the firm has power in at least one of those markets.[22]

The most common examples of the tying contract can readily be shown to be devices permitting the firm to discriminate with respect to price in the sale of the product over which it has some degree of monopoly control.[23]

[21] See William J. Baumol, *Business Behavior, Value and Growth* (New York: Macmillan, 1959), esp. pp. 45-82; Oliver E. Williamson, *The Economics of Discretionary Behavior: Managerial Objectives in a Theory of the Firm* (Englewood Cliffs: Prentice-Hall, 1964), esp. pp. 1-27, and J. Williamson, "Profit, Growth and Sales Maximization," *Economica*, Vol. 33, February 1966, pp. 1-16.

[22] Where the price of a product is externally controlled—as, for example, under wartime price control—tying the sale of the price-controlled product to the purchase of an item whose price is not controlled can, of course, be an effective device for avoiding that control.

[23] See James M. Ferguson, "Tying Arrangements and Reciprocity: An Economic Analysis," in Werner Sichel, *Industrial Organization and Public Policy* (Boston: Houghton Mifflin, 1967), pp. 285-300, and M. L. Burstein, "A Theory of Full-Line Forcing," *Northwestern University Law Review*, Vol. 55, March-April 1960, pp. 62-95.

The tied product serves essentially as a "counter" determining the effective price for the tying product. Not only is it not clear that the resulting multiple-price system for the tying product is not socially preferable to the alternative single profit-maximizing price for that product, but it is also generally true that "counters" can be devised which generate closely similar sets of prices without the tie to the tied product.[24] The present price policy followed by Xerox in the leasing of its office copiers provides a nice illustration in this regard in comparison with the earlier tying contracts imposed by IBM in the leasing of tabulating equipment.[25] But quite apart from this, the tying contract makes no sense in the absence of monopoly or near monopoly position in at least one market, cannot be shown to be more than an effective pricing device *in* that market, and, if a problem, is a problem in terms of market structure, not corporate size.[26]

[24] Ferguson, in fact, suggests that ". . . in some cases . . . the meter might be the more efficient method of discrimination." James M. Ferguson, *op.cit.*, p. 290.

[25] Rates for office-copying equipment are based not only on the number of copies made but also on the number of duplicate copies made at the same time. For example, the charge is less for 10 copies of the same page (made at the same time) than for 10 single copies of 10 different pages, even though the cost (to Xerox) would appear to be virtually identical. This may be a rather cute illustration of "value of service" pricing, which is, of course, a form of price discrimination. See also *International Business Machines*, sv U.S. 298, U.S. 131 (1936).

[26] There, of course, may be other reasons for the use of a tying contract. One was noted earlier—the avoidance of price control. But the device may, in some instances, be a quite legitimate means of protecting the integrity of a product. In the early stages of the introduction of color film, for example, the tying of processing to the purchase of the film might have been thought desirable solely to guarantee the film's performance. In other

Exclusive Dealing

Exclusive dealing can, on the one hand, be closely similar to the tying contract in its effect and motivation. Miller, for example, has argued that exclusive contracts by petroleum refiners with their distributors regarding tires, batteries, and accessories are consistent with the discriminatory sale of branded petroleum products.[27] The same explanation presumably underlies most enforced or attempted ties in the case of franchised distributors—the General Motors–General Motors Acceptance Corporation tie, for example.[28] On the other hand, the exclusive

---

instances (or in that one), the practice may also serve to conceal technical information making entry by outsiders to the industry of the tying product more difficult. The discriminatory pricing implicit in the use of a tied product as a counter (or meter, in Ferguson's terms) may also have the effect of creating an additional barrier to entry to the market of the tying product. (Note that insofar as the device increases the profitability of manufacture, it may also provide an added incentive to entry.) But these as well are problems of market structure—imperfection in the structure of the market for the tying product—not related to size of firm and not, in the absence of that market imperfection, to the operation of a firm in more than one market.

[27] See Richard A. Miller, "Exclusive Dealing in the Petroleum Industry," *Yale Economic Essays*, No. 1, 1963, pp. 223-247.

[28] Suppose, for example, that the earnings of automobile dealers come in part from the financing of automobile purchases. Suppose further that the proportion of automobile sales that are financed varies from dealer to dealer. If the terms of transfer, between manufacturer and dealer, of automobiles is independent of the proportion of subsequent sales that are financed, then the franchise will be worth more, other things being equal, to the dealer for whom more retail sales are financed. Some of the economic rent (created by the manufacturer's franchise) can therefore be appropriated by the manufacturer if such financing is handled exclusively by the manufacturer or his subsidiary.

contract may also make sense from the seller's standpoint in cases where salesmanship is an important component of consumer acceptance but where controlled or franchised outlets are not attractive. The Standard Fashions contracts involving dress patterns are the best-known illustration. In this setting, the practice is analogous to seller-enforced resale price maintenance.[29] But in general, the issue is not leverage but rather the desirability of particular forms of multiple pricing or of non-price competition, neither of which would arise in the absence of market power and neither of which is a feature of the *large* corporation *per se*.

Multiple Pricing

Perhaps the most striking aspect of all these restrictive arrangements is the degree to which the advantage of discriminatory pricing provides a ready explanation. And there is nothing in economic theory more misleading than the widespread assumption of a single price for a given product, and the emphasis given to the concept of marginal revenue under that assumption. *There is probably no firm with any appreciable degree of market power that does not discriminate in some way in the sale of its product.* Indeed, this probably is the basis not only for much of the incentive leading to the vertical integration of firms in many areas of fabrication (as Bork has argued), but also for what has come to be known as reciprocal buying.[30] Many industrial markets are highly con-

[29] Standard Fashion Co. v. Magrabe-Houston Co., 258 U.S. 346 (1922). Where exclusive agencies are not feasible (as, for example, in the case of many smaller specialty items including cosmetics), rigidly enforced resale price maintenance may be an alternative way of securing identity of interest between seller and manufacturer.

[30] See Robert Bork, "Vertical Integration and the Sherman

centrated. Where products in those markets are at all standardized, prices will tend to be rigid, and the competition of firms will emphasize various non-price techniques. Under those circumstances, product prices will tend to exceed marginal production and distribution costs. It will be advantageous to individual firms to make additional sales, but open use of price as a device to achieve that end will be unlikely. That is not to say that price cuts—or price competition—will not occur, but only that firms will tend to make price concessions, or their equivalent, when such concessions can be concealed and be made applicable only to marginal sales. Many forms of non-price competition—freight absorption, for example—can readily be viewed in this fashion, and a good case can be made that reciprocal dealing among large firms is exactly this kind of behavior in disguise.[31]

Reciprocal Dealing

For example, suppose two firms each operate in (different) markets where products are reasonably standardized and where the usual conditions and consequences of oligopoly are present. Prevailing prices substantially ex-

---

Act: The Legal History of an Economic Misconception," *Chicago Law Review*, 1954, pp. 157-201. Bork's analysis, however, implicitly assumes fixed factor proportions. That assumption is critical to his argument. The existence of variable proportions provides a basis for the "leverage" Bork seeks to deny. See the very interesting conclusions of Richard Schmalensee, "A Note on the Theory of Vertical Integration," *Journal of Political Economy*, Vol. 81, March-April 1973, pp. 442-449. Schmalensee does not show it, but his analysis is equally applicable to a wide range of restrictive practice, including tying and exclusive contracts.

[31] See, for example, James M. Ferguson, *loc. cit.*, esp. pp. 303-309. Ferguson's argument, in part, is very similar to that presented here.

ceed marginal cost; firms are highly (non-price) competitive; no single firm dominates either market. Suppose further that each of the two firms is a *potential* customer of the other. Under these circumstances, each firm would benefit from expanding its sales by converting the other firm from a potential to an *actual* customer; each firm would profit from such added sales even at prices substantially below prevailing levels. In short, each firm would presumably like to be able to price selectively—to discriminate—to acquire added sales, but is unlikely to be able to do so. Open concessions in price could be matched immediately by competing firms and would be likely to lead to a general and unprofitable decline in prices over all.

Reciprocal dealing, however, offers a device by which such a concession can be made without the likelihood of retaliation. Suppose the two firms in the example above agree to buy from each other rather than from competitors. The purchase price to each becomes, if the two accounts cancel, the *relative* price of the two goods.[32] If in each market price exceeds marginal cost by the same relative amount, the effect is as though each firm had sold to the other at a price equal to marginal production cost—perfectly competitive terms for those transactions. Barter would have replaced dealing at established market prices.

The incentive to that barter is that prevailing prices do not accurately measure actual costs, and hence barter can provide a mutually advantageous result for both parties. The key, of course, is that there must be com-

---

[32] In money terms, the purchase price to either firm will be the ratio of the price of its trading partner's product to the price of its own product, times the marginal cost of its own product. This, of course, will be strictly correct only if the reciprocal purchases exactly cancel each other at market prices.

petitors in *both* markets; otherwise the two transactions cannot be considered to be offsetting as in the preceding example. It is also necessary that the two markets in question be imperfect. No such gain can be shown for reciprocal dealing between perfectly competitive firms.

What this suggests is that reciprocal dealing can be viewed as a response to market imperfection.[33] The effect will obviously benefit the reciprocal dealers to the detriment of their competitors, just as would equivalent price concessions. Price concessions, however, should lead rather promptly to more competitive price levels in the market as a whole, and hence would be more desirable; but the whole framework of oligopoly theory suggests that such concessions are not likely, although they are perhaps more likely than at least some of the literature would imply.[34]

But reciprocal dealing will also place a competitive pressure on the markets involved. The competitors of the reciprocal dealers will be placed at a disadvantage. Their alternative is also to find a partner for such an arrangement, which is not apt to be likely, or to price more competitively in order to reduce the incentive to reciprocity.[35]

[33] This response can be considered "competitive" only in the sense that a selective price concession, brought about by the threat of the transfer of purchases to another seller, is competitive. As in the case of quantity discounts, prohibition of the practice *might* lead to a general reduction in price levels. Then again, it might have the opposite effect, and tend only to eliminate one source of pressure toward price flexibility in concentrated industries.

[34] See George J. Stigler and James K. Kindahl, *The Behavior of Industrial Prices* (New York: National Bureau of Economic Research, 1970).

[35] Note that this argument suggests that reciprocity may be an important motive underlying some conglomerate acquisitions. It

However, the basic economic problem is not reciprocity but the imperfection of market structure that leads to it. If market structure is not to be improved—and there is not a great deal of encouraging evidence during the past twenty years—it is far from obvious that reciprocity is a totally bad thing. It is analogous to discriminating monopoly.

It is perfectly true that the larger a firm, and the more (imperfect) intermediate markets in which that firm is involved, the greater will be the possibilities for reciprocity.[36] The practice contains the basis for a relative advantage for the large multiproduct firm. If corporate size and pervasiveness are regarded as undesirable *per se*, they can be discouraged by the banning of reciprocal dealing. But in the face of continuing oligopoly in many markets the cost could be the elimination of one source of pressure towards a more competitive behavior in those markets.[37]

---

also provides a rationale for denying such acquisitions. That rationale, however, depends heavily on assumptions with regard to industry dynamics, about which very little is known or can be said. The argument, however, also suggests that the time to block this kind of conglomerate acquisition is *after* some reciprocal dealing has become characteristic of the markets in question.

[36] See Federal Trade Commission, *op.cit.*, pp. 7-8 and 394-397. It is interesting that the illustrations of reciprocal dealing provided by the Commission's report appear in general to conform, in their setting, to that suggested here as being conducive to the practice. See pp. 338-393.

[37] Note the similarity between this analysis of reciprocal dealing and Bork's analysis of the economic effects of vertical integration and mergers. See Robert Bork, *op.cit.*, pp. 157-201. Both vertical integration and reciprocity also have the effect of lessening access to intermediate markets, and hence may tend to lessen the likelihood of entry by new firms. This Bork by and large ignores, and the Federal Trade Commission *Report* stresses. See Federal Trade Commission, *op.cit.*, pp. 7 and 328-330. The

And the presence of reciprocal dealing among large corporations does not establish the economic undesirability of the large corporation. The causality, if any, is the reverse.[38]

THE TREND TOWARD BIGNESS

What does it all add up to? First, as Adelman said twenty years ago, the American economy is highly concentrated.[39] Second, every indication is that it became more so during the past twenty years.[40] Third, these large

---

basic similarity between the conglomerate merger and the vertical merger is discussed again, and in more detail, in Chapter VII below.

[38] That is, if the large corporation is undesirable, it follows that reciprocity is undesirable to the extent that the practice provides a relative advantage to the large firm.

[39] M. A. Adelman, "The Measurement of Industrial Concentration," Review of Economics and Statistics, Vol. 33, November 1951, p. 295.

[40] Two aspects of this increase should be noted. First, within the largest industrials, the relative position of the very largest has declined. In 1954, the 25 largest industrials (in terms of sales) held 41.9 percent of the total assets of the 500 largest. In 1968, that percentage was 38.8. Corresponding figures for the 10 largest are 27.4 and 24.3. See Sanford Rose, "Bigness is a Numbers Game," *Fortune*, Vol. 80, November 1969, p. 238. The other aspect of this changing corporate structure is, of course, that the largest corporations of one period are not necessarily the largest of another period. There is turnover among and within the largest. A rather interesting demonstration of this has recently been provided by Mermelstein, who relates the relative asset share of individual large corporations from one period to another between 1909 and 1964. With the exception of the 10-year interval of 1948 to 1958, a decline in the size of the individual corporation relative to his sample of large corporations is predicted. Mermelstein also finds, however, that this trend toward relative decline consistently diminishes during the

corporations represent a combination of wealth and social power that is privately controlled and not in any real sense publicly accountable. In the past, and certainly at present, the charge is made that significant political decisions are made in accordance with the dictates of this industrial establishment. That may be correct. It is not, however, the normal focus of economic analysis.[41]

Within economics, the significance of corporate size is based on *market* position—relative size *within* individual markets—not on any trend or standard of relative corporate size within the industrial sector (or even the economy) as a whole. It is partly for that reason that Sanford Rose dubbed corporate bigness a numbers game.[42] And it is. But corporate bigness is also a fact, and it appears that it is going to remain a fact. That is perhaps the major implication. Analysis of the economic performance of U.S. industry will in very large part be analysis of the performance of a few hundred corporations. It is here that the major gains or losses of future economic policy will be felt. Whether those are gains or losses will correspondingly depend on the implications of that policy for the relative position (or power) of these large firms within the individual markets of industry. It is about recent change in this regard that little is known or documented. It cannot be inferred from simple tabulations of the corporate structure of industry.

55-year period, with the implication that the rate of turnover among large corporations is tending to decline. See David Mermelstein, "Large Industrial Corporations and Asset Shares," *American Economic Review*, Vol. 59, September 1969, pp. 431-451.

[41] For an elegant statement in this regard, see Carl Kaysen and Donald F. Turner, *Antitrust Policy: An Economic and Legal Analysis* (Cambridge: Harvard University Press, 1959), pp. 17-18.

[42] Sanford Rose, *op.cit.*, p. 113.

III

Inter-industry Aspects of Corporate Concentration

CHAPTER II emphasized the role of market structure, as opposed to corporate size, in assessing the structural imperfection of American industry. It does not, however, follow that recent change in the corporate concentration of industry has had no effect on the market power of leading firms within concentrated industries. It is only that any such effect is not obvious.[1] Indeed, the theme of this chapter, and the rationale for much of the following empirical analysis, is that increasing corporate concentration of the kind that occurred in the United States during the past twenty or twenty-five years could have led to either a substantial increase or a substantial decrease in the market power of leading firms in national markets. It depends on the source or the nature of the relative growth by these largest corporations.

SOURCES OF CORPORATE GROWTH

For example, suppose that over a twenty-year period, the largest few firms in each of the individual industries of manufacturing and mining were to grow *within* those industries—to improve their market position relative to their smaller competitors. Suppose further that these firms

[1] This argument is also developed in Charles H. Berry, "Corporate Bigness and Diversification in Manufacturing," *Ohio State Law Journal*, Vol. 28, No. 3, 1967, pp. 402-426.

were also, generally, the largest industrial corporations over all—that the leading firms in industrial markets were also the largest firms. The corporate structure of industry would become increasingly concentrated, and the implication would be that market structure had become increasingly imperfect with the market power of leading firms being increased.

That does not appear to have been the actual basis—certainly not the exclusive basis—for the relative growth by the largest industrials documented earlier. Increasing corporate concentration of manufacturing since 1947 has not been accompanied by a corresponding increase in the average level of the concentration of the various component industries of manufacturing.[2] The increasing concentration of some industries has been by and large offset by decreasing concentration in others.[3] Any expansion in the market shares of large corporations contributing to their relative growth appears to have come, at least in part, within industries in which those firms were not among the 4 largest sellers.

Alternatively, however, market imperfection within industry would also have to be considered to have increased if the largest industrial corporations could be shown to have grown as a consequence of more rapid than average growth by concentrated *industries*. The largest industrial corporations tend to be those with lead-

[2] For 213 4-digit industries for which this information is available, average 4-firm concentration was 41.2 percent in 1947 and 41.8 percent in 1966. See *Studies by the Staff of the Cabinet Committee on Price Stability* (Government Printing Office, January 1969), p. 58.

[3] *Ibid.* Concentration ratios (4-firm) rose by more than 3 percentage points in 88 of 213 4-digit industries between 1947 and 1966, but also declined by more than 3 percentage points in 78 of those 4-digit industries.

ing market position in concentrated industries. If those industries grew relative to others, and if market shares remained unchanged, relative growth by large firms would have been the result.

The evidence on this score is ambiguous. If the industries that are highly concentrated are also those tending to grow most rapidly, the average concentration of all industries, when that average is unweighted, should show a tendency to decline relative to the average concentration ratio obtained when industries are weighted by their relative size. There is some supporting evidence in this regard, but precise results vary with the particular industries included and with the manner in which industries are weighted by their relative size. There is the further difficulty, here and also in the earlier example, that information is available for only a very limited number of the component industries of manufacturing.[4] On neither question is the evidence as satisfactory as would be desired.

It is, however, clear that relative growth by large corporations could reflect, and indeed has reflected, an increase in the number of industries in which these firms are active. This trend is developed in detail by the F.T.C. *Economic Report on Corporate Mergers*. It is shown rather dramatically by Table 3-1, reproduced from that report. The issue here is the significance of that kind of diversification to the behavior of the industrial markets involved. And that again is not obvious.

[4] See F. M. Scherer, *Industrial Market Structure and Industry Performance* (Chicago: Rand McNally, 1970), pp. 60-63. Scherer shows that weighted (by value added) average concentration in 1947 was higher with 1963 weights than with 1947 weights by about 2.6 percentage points, but the comparison is based on fewer than half the total number of 4-digit industries in both years.

TABLE 3-1:

AVERAGE NUMBER OF PRODUCTION CATEGORIES IN WHICH THE
200 LARGEST MANUFACTURING COMPANIES OPERATED
DURING 1960, 1965 AND 1968

Production Category	Average Number of Product Categories of the 200 Largest Manufacturing Companies [a]		
	1960	1965	1968
5-digit Product Classes	21	27	33
4-digit Industries	13	16	20
3-digit Minor Industry Groups	9	11	14
2-digit Major Industry Groups	4	5	6

[a] Ranked by assets

Source: Federal Trade Commission, *Economic Report on Corporate Mergers*, Staff Report to the Federal Trade Commission (Government Printing Office, 1969), p. 221.

Barriers to Entry

Market concentration is conducive to oligopoly behavior where such markets are protected at least temporarily from the entry of competing firms.[5] Apart from legislated barriers—patents, licenses, and the like—the more important barriers to entry can generally be traced to some form of scale economy. That could be economy of scale in production, as in aluminum for example, but increasingly more important are economies of mass communi-

[5] The point should be obvious, but for a clear discussion relating entry barriers to the measurement of industrial concentration, see Tibor Scitovsky, "Economic Theory and the Measurement of Concentration," in National Bureau of Economic Research, *Business Concentration and Price Policy* (Princeton: Princeton University Press, 1955), pp. 101-118. See also Dean A. Worcester, "Why Dominant Firms Decline," *Journal of Political Economy*, Vol. 65, August 1957, pp. 338-347.

cation and merchandising that have developed as regional and local markets have been absorbed within broader national markets for many industrial products.[6]

Where the nature of markets is such that the nationally known organization, or simply the large industrial producer, has an inherent competitive advantage, entry, if it does occur, is more likely on the part of a large organization where the necessary size, familiarity, or needed control of financial resources has already been attained.[7]

To put it slightly differently, the most likely, and certainly the most potent, entrant to a large concentrated national market is a large corporation that is already active on a national basis. If barriers to entry are generally, or even frequently, a consequence of corporate size, those barriers will be broken most easily by those firms for whom a lack of size is not a debilitating factor.[8]

[6] See, for example, the discussion in F. M. Scherer, *op.cit.*, pp. 95-103. See also Charles H. Berry, "Economic Policy and the Conglomerate Merger," *St. John's Law Review*, Vol. 44, Special Edition, Spring 1970, pp. 260-281, esp. pp. 269-273.

[7] For an interesting examination of the relationship between the cost of equity capital and corporate size, see S. H. Archer and L. G. Faerber, "Firm Size and the Cost of Externally Acquired Equity Capital," *Journal of Finance*, March 1966, pp. 69-83.

[8] Joe S. Bain, evaluating entry barriers in 20 selected manufacturing industries put it this way: ". . . absolute capital requirements for an efficient plant in all the manufacturing industries examined are large enough to restrict seriously the ranks of potential entrants; even 500,000 dollars, the smallest amount listed, will not be forthcoming from savings out of salary or from the winnings in a poker game." (And note the reference is to a single plant.) J. S. Bain, "Economies of Scale, Concentration, and the Condition of Entry in Twenty Manufacturing Industries," in American Economic Association, *Readings in Industrial Organization and Public Policy* (Homewood: Richard D. Irwin, 1958), p. 67.

Recent relative growth by large industrial corporations has been accompanied by an increase in the number of industries in which those firms are active. If this increased diversification has contributed to that growth, then such growth may be consistent, not with the creation of even greater barriers to entry in national markets, but with a reduced significance of those entry barriers which already exist. In this view, relative growth has been accompanied by the development of diversified corporations with both the necessary size and the will to cross industry lines wherever that is expected to be advantageous. In the light of tax law favoring the corporate retention of industrial earnings, and with a very high percentage of gross private capital formation in industry originating from the retained earnings of the 500 largest industrial firms, that is presumably the way in which one would *want* the largest industrial corporations to behave.

Unfortunately, however, the diversification recorded in Table 3-1, and the corporate growth that has accompanied it, is equally consistent with diversification that tends to consolidate within single corporations market position in competing or potentially competing industries, with the result that the regulatory force of entry or potential entry is reduced, not increased.[9]

This can be argued in several ways. Perhaps the clearest is in the case of directly competing industries. Diversification by a glass container corporation by acquisition of a manufacturer of plastic containers would expand the

[9] There is a hint of this in the finding by the Federal Trade Commission that acquisitions by large firms tend heavily to be firms active within the same 2-digit industry group. See *Economic Report on Corporate Mergers*, Staff Report to the Federal Trade Commission (Government Printing Office, 1969), pp. 242-247.

firm's market share in the container field. At the 4-digit level it would be shown as diversification in Table 3-1, and would not by itself affect the recorded structure of either industry. Similarly, much of the increasing diversification at the 2-digit level shown in Table 3-1 may reflect vertical consolidation. The merger of a major steel producer and a leading manufacturer of automobiles would similarly result in corporate growth and apparent diversification but without any implication that the structure of either market had been improved, and with the certain implication that one potentially competitive force in the steel industry had been removed.

Corporate Diversification and Market Structure

The obvious conclusion is that the term "diversification" without further qualification means little. Firms may diversify with various consequences. The essential questions relate to what the implications of that diversification are in terms of market structure, and in the way that market structure is itself defined. The largest industrial corporations in the United States are both relatively larger and more diversified than they were twenty years ago. It is not clear, however, what kind of diversification has been related to this relative growth by large corporations. It is quite possible that diversification and growth indicate an increasing degree of effective inter-industry competition among those (and other) firms; it is also possible that they reflect chiefly an increasing consolidation of market power within a relatively few large firms. But no evidence in either direction is provided by the finding that large firms are relatively larger and more diversified.

The remainder of this book reports an attempt to provide at least preliminary evidence bearing on this distinction. The analysis is in three parts. First, the turnover of the plant facilities of these larger industrial corporations is examined—the potential inter-industry activity of the 500 largest. This is followed by the development of indices of diversification and of changing diversification for these corporations, and a statistical analysis of the link between corporate growth and this process of industrial diversification by large firms. Finally, measures of change in the concentration in individual manufacturing industries are related to the entry into and exit from those industries by these same approximately 500 largest industrial corporations. In each case, an effort is made to assess the impact on market structure of the inter-industry activity of large industrial firms.

The Data

Appropriate data for this purpose are not readily available. Ideally, Bureau of the Census establishment records, aggregated by companies over time, could be used to obtain a comprehensive picture contrasting the behavior of large manufacturing firms with that of firms of other size with respect not only to growth and diversification but also to relative position within the various individual industries of manufacturing. The Bureau of the Census has the data to permit this kind of analysis; Census disclosure rules prevent their availability to non-Census analysts.

As the next best alternative, data relating to the products and change in the products of the largest industrials have been taken from the 1961 and 1966 editions of the Plant and Product Directory prepared by *Fortune*. An appendix to this chapter outlines the procedure followed in the processing and assembly of these data, and notes their major limitations. The industrial corporations considered are 494 of the 500 largest, in terms of sales, in

1960.[10] Between 1960 and 1965, the time interval of this analysis, thirty of these corporations disappeared by merger with another of the corporations in this group, one was liquidated, and two ceased domestic manufacturing activity. The 494 largest in 1960 were therefore reduced to 461 independent successor corporations in 1965.[11]

The major drawback is that, in contrast to the confidential Census data, these Fortune data permit no analysis of the role of corporate acquisitions in the changing diversification of these large industrial corporations. Nor is it possible to combine these data with other records to eliminate this deficiency. The 30 mergers within the group are discussed briefly below, but beyond that the contribution of corporate mergers to the plant composition of these 461 corporations remains speculative. That contribution is undoubtedly large, but how large or of what sort cannot in any way be determined from these data. The advantage of the data is that they document plant-product combinations over time within corporations. But the basis of the acquisition of new plants, or the fate of plants disappearing from the sample, is not indicated.

PLANTS OF THE LARGEST INDUSTRIALS

In 1960 the original 494 largest industrials reported (to *Fortune*) 10,181 separate plant facilities.[12] In 1965 the 461 successors to those 494 reported a total of 11,618,

---

[10] Data were unavailable for the 6 of the 500 largest. See Chapter III, Appendix.

[11] These mergers are identified in Chapter III, Appendix.

[12] All characteristics of these corporations cited subsequently are, unless otherwise indicated, from *Fortune, Market Research Department, 1961 Plant and Product Directory* (Time, Inc., 1961) or the *1966 Plant and Product Directory* (Time, Inc., 1966).

an increase of about 15 percent. That increase markedly understates the turnover in these establishments. Of the initial 10,181 in 1960, only 7,923 could be identified (by plant address) among the plants reported by these firms in 1965.[13]

The 7,923 plants identified in both 1960 and 1965 are here referred to as "matched plants." Their records were matched over the five-year period. "Unmatched plants" are those for which records were available in 1965 but not 1960 (added plants) or, conversely, those for which records were available in 1960 but not in 1965 (dropped plants).

Plant Turnover

Table 3-2 shows the distribution of all plants by number of employees in 1960 and in 1965 as well as the size dis-

TABLE 3-2:

NUMBER OF PLANTS OF THE 494-461 FORTUNE CORPORATIONS
BY NUMBER OF EMPLOYEES, 1960 AND 1965

	Number of Plants			
Number of *Employees*	Total 1960	Total 1965	Added 1960-1965	Dropped 1960-1965
1-99	2,087	3,304	1,415	669
100-499	2,835	3,505	1,035	503
500-999	776	983	191	103
1,000-4,999	752	1,023	164	86
Over 5,000	101	157	21	7
Unknown	3,630	2,646	869	890[a]
Total	10,181	11,618	3,695	2,258

[a] Includes 48 plants "sold" to corporations among the 1,000 largest in 1965, but not among the 461 Fortune corporations.

Source: Fortune, 1961 Plant and Product Directory (Time, Inc., 1961) and 1966 Plant and Product Directory (Time, Inc., 1966).

[13] Of the 7,923 identified, 288 were reported by different corporations in the two years.

41

tribution of those plants added or dropped over the five-year period. As would be expected, the table suggests that turnover of plant facilities was heavily concentrated among the smaller plants.

That turnover, however, was the basis for a substantial amount of inter-industry movement by these firms. Table 3-3 shows the total number of instances in which one of these plants entered or left a 2-digit industry group, together with the total number of the plants of these corporations active in these 2-digit industry groups in 1960 and 1965. Table 3-4 contains an equivalent tabulation, but for matched plants only—those which were among the plants reported by the largest industrials in both 1960 *and* 1965. Table 3-5 shows this entry and exit at the 2-digit level separately for matched and unmatched plants. Table 3-6 gives corresponding data for a few selected 4-digit industries.

In each of these tables, a plant is counted once for each industry in which it reported one or more products. Totals therefore exceed the actual number of plants, and correspond instead to the number of plant-product combinations.

Two conclusions are apparent at this point. *First*, as is clear from Table 3-5, the most important component of this inter-industry activity can be traced to the turnover of actual plants—to the *unmatched* plants in Table 3-5. By itself, that finding is ambiguous. On the one hand, it is to be expected. A new plant—one that was present in 1965 but not in 1960—is by definition an entering plant. Similarly, a dropped plant is an exiting plant. All unmatched plants therefore *must* result in plant entry or exit. Furthermore, entry or expansion into a totally new area of productive endeavor on the part of any firm is presumably far more likely to involve the acquisition of a new facility than the conversion of an existing one. It should be clear, on the other hand, that this *plant* entry and exit by no means necessarily involves *corporate* entry and exit. For example, if the plants of all corporations were periodically relocated as a matter of course—per-

TABLE 3-3:

ENTRY AND EXIT BY PLANTS OF THE 494-461 FORTUNE
CORPORATIONS, 2-DIGIT INDUSTRY GROUPS, 1960 AND 1965

Industry Code	Total Number of Fortune Plants 1960	1965	Plants Entering Number	Percent of 1960	Plants Exiting Number	Percent of 1960
10	53	62	20	37.7	11	20.8
11	6	41	40	666.7	5	83.3
12	52	74	32	61.5	10	19.2
13	74	132	72	97.3	14	13.5
14	146	212	105	71.9	39	26.7
19	106	116	59	55.7	49	46.2
20	2,260	2,229	591	26.2	622	27.5
21	24	27	5	20.8	2	8.3
22	454	490	105	23.1	69	15.2
23	93	158	85	91.4	20	21.5
24	273	312	129	47.3	90	33.0
25	65	93	48	73.8	20	30.8
26	903	1,009	320	35.4	214	23.7
27	133	170	83	62.4	46	34.6
28	1,722	2,066	766	44.5	422	24.5
29	309	378	135	43.7	66	21.4
30	287	461	264	92.0	90	31.4
31	178	149	19	10.7	48	27.0
32	744	722	206	27.7	228	30.6
33	679	739	199	29.3	139	20.5
34	846	973	359	42.4	232	27.4
35	876	1,042	439	50.1	273	31.2
36	815	1,008	462	56.7	269	33.0
37	567	660	258	45.5	165	29.1
38	218	292	166	76.1	92	42.2
39	103	113	54	52.4	44	42.7
93	6	15	11	183.3	2	33.3
95	0	6	6	–	0	–
99	8	125	119	1,487.5	2	25.0
Total	12,000	13,874	5,157	42.9	3,283	27.3

Source: Same as Table 3-2.

haps as part of the general process of urban development —and if all corporations tended over time to add to build additional plants, this same general pattern of plant entry and exit would appear even if there were no change in the product mix of any corporation.

TABLE 3-4:

ENTRY AND EXIT BY PLANTS OF THE 494-461 FORTUNE CORPORATIONS 2-DIGIT INDUSTRY GROUPS, 1960 AND 1965— *Matched Plants Only*

Industry Code	Number of Matched Plants		Matched Plants Entering		Matched Plants Exiting	
	1960	1965	Number	Percent of 1960	Number	Percent of 1960
10	45	45	3	6.7	3	6.7
11	2	1	0	0.0	1	50.0
12	42	43	1	2.4	0	0.0
13	63	65	5	7.9	3	4.8
14	114	121	14	12.3	7	6.1
19	76	74	17	22.4	19	25.0
20	1,653	1,652	14	0.8	15	0.9
21	22	22	0	0.0	0	0.0
22	393	399	14	3.6	8	2.0
23	78	102	29	37.2	5	6.4
24	191	206	23	12.0	8	4.2
25	48	54	9	18.8	3	6.3
26	763	730	41	5.4	74	9.7
27	94	93	6	6.4	7	7.4
28	1,385	1,375	75	5.4	85	6.1
29	270	259	16	5.9	27	10.0
30	231	260	63	27.3	34	14.7
31	141	135	5	3.5	11	7.8
32	542	552	36	6.6	26	4.8
33	570	576	36	6.3	30	5.3
34	666	690	76	11.4	52	7.8
35	669	693	90	13.5	66	9.9
36	594	619	73	12.3	48	8.1
37	445	477	75	16.9	43	9.7
38	161	169	43	26.7	35	21.7
39	73	69	10	13.7	14	19.2
93	5	7	3	60.0	1	20.0
95	0	1	1	–	0	–
99	7	44	38	542.9	1	14.3
Total	9,343	9,533	816	8.7	626	6.7

Source: Same as Table 3-2.

44

Second, however, the documented plant turnover is sufficiently high so that it suggests much more than this kind of purely secular development. Apart from the obvious questions of errors and inaccuracies in this particular data set—discussed in the appendix to this chapter—any

TABLE 3-5:

NUMBER OF PLANTS OF THE 494-461 FORTUNE CORPORATIONS, ENTRY AND EXIT BY 2-DIGIT INDUSTRY GROUPS, 1960 AND 1965

Industry Code	Total Plants Present		Plants Entering		Plants Exiting	
	1960	1965	Matched	Unmatched	Matched	Unmatched
10	53	62	3	17	3	8
11	6	41	0	40	1	4
12	52	74	1	31	0	10
13	74	132	5	67	3	11
14	146	212	14	91	7	32
19	106	116	17	42	19	30
20	2,260	2,229	14	577	15	607
21	24	27	0	5	0	2
22	454	490	14	91	8	61
23	93	158	29	56	5	15
24	273	312	23	106	8	82
25	65	93	9	39	3	17
26	903	1,009	41	279	74	140
27	133	170	6	77	7	39
28	1,722	2,066	75	691	85	337
29	309	378	16	119	27	39
30	287	461	63	201	34	56
31	178	149	5	14	11	37
32	744	722	36	170	26	202
33	679	739	36	163	30	109
34	846	973	76	283	52	180
35	876	1,042	90	349	66	207
36	815	1,008	73	389	48	221
37	567	660	75	183	43	122
38	218	292	43	123	35	57
39	103	113	10	44	14	30
93	6	15	3	8	1	1
95	0	6	1	5	0	0
99	8	125	38	81	1	1
Total	12,000	13,874	816	4,341	626	2,657

Source: Same as Table 3-2.

TABLE 3-6:

MANUFACTURING PLANTS OF THE 494-461 FORTUNE
CORPORATIONS, BY SELECTED 4-DIGIT INDUSTRY, AND
STATUS OF THE PLANT IN 1960 AND 1965

4-digit Industry		*Plants Present, 1960 and 1965 with Products in This Industry Group*			*Plants Present, 1960 or 1965, with Products in This Industry Group*	
		(1)	(2)	(3)	(4)	(5)
		1960				
	SIC	and	1960	1965		
Name	Code	1965	Only	Only	1960	1965
Meat Packing	(2011)	34	70	1	22	17
Malt Liquors	(2082)	16	0	0	1	1
Cigarettes	(2111)	11	0	0	1	1
Broad Woven Cotton	(2211)	112	38	6	14	31
Men's Suits, Coats, Overcoats	(2311)	16	0	4	1	6
Veneer & Plywood	(2432)	33	7	4	16	39
Wood Furniture	(2512)	10	1	0	1	6
Paper Mills	(2621)	90	13	6	17	44
Book Publishing	(2731)	55	1	0	3	7
Biological Drugs	(2831)	19	5	6	5	17
Gum and Wood Chemicals	(2861)	8	2	10	2	11
Oils and Grease	(2992)	8	2	6	4	6
Tires and Tubes	(3011)	33	2	1	3	15
Industrial Leather Belting	(3121)	2	2	0	0	0
Flat Glass	(3211)	20	1	1	0	4
Steel Pipes, etc.	(3317)	16	8	4	8	9
Metal Cans	(3411)	126	3	4	23	43
Elevators, etc.	(3534)	3	1	3	1	2
Electrical Instruments	(3611)	22	11	10	16	35
Aircraft Engines & Parts	(3722)	49	10	13	16	31
Laboratory Instruments	(3811)	22	12	9	25	51

Source: Same as Table 3-2.

number of hypotheses can be advanced. Casual examination of the raw data gives the impression of significant regional shifts. More interesting would be tests to identify turnover that is attributable to urban growth and suburban industrial development. The data would permit such an analysis. Shifts in the degree of vertical integration within plants could explain some of the plant disappearance. Again, with suitable manipulation, the detail of these data would permit analysis at that level. The list could be expanded.

Here, however, the emphasis is on the inter-industry activity, over all, of these 461 firms. The plant data show substantial turnover. Whatever else may be suggested, the data at this level indicate a correspondingly high degree of potential inter-industry activity by the corporations themselves. At the plant level, and as a whole, these corporations show a surprisingly large amount of entry and exit from what would appear to be distinct and independent markets. That aspect of the data is the primary focus of what follows.

A NOTE ON MERGERS

Between 1960 and 1965, of the 494 largest industrial corporations in 1960, 33 disappeared by merger, by liquidation (which is clearly a form of merger since assets are sold, though presumably not to a single buyer), and by exit from domestic manufacturing (a process under which assets are presumably also sold). Straightforward merger accounted for 30 of the 33 disappearances, and all but one were absorbed by corporations among the original 494.[14]

[14] See Chapter III, Appendix. Daystrom was acquired by Schlumberger in 1962. Schlumberger was not classified as an

The 33 corporations that disappeared had reported a total of 497 separate plants in 1960. Of these, 252 were not among the plants reported by the successor 461 corporations in 1965. Of the 245 remaining, 29 were no longer active at all in the 2-digit industry group in which they had been active five years earlier, and in a further 47 instances these plants had entered a new 2-digit industry group—that is, they were manufacturing products in a new 2-digit industry group while still remaining active in the original 2-digit category. Table 3-7 shows this detail at the 2-digit level. Table 3-8 provides corresponding totals at the 3- and 4-digit levels.

Both tables indicate very much more entry and exit by the plants of these merged corporations than by all plants of the large corporations. This is especially true if the comparison is restricted, for the merged corporations, to those plants present in both 1960 and 1965. While no attempt has been made to classify these mergers by type or motive, the record suggests that they were not instrumental, at least not uniformly so, either in the consolidation of market position within particular industries or in the acquisition of market position within industries for the acquiring firm. The disappearance of half of the plants of the merged firms, and the very high rate of exit and entry that is characteristic of the plants that remained, is far more consistent with a heavy element of liquidation in these mergers among large firms.

Two comments must, however, be added. First, for these merged corporations it is far more likely than for the sample as a whole that changes in the definition of plants, or their reported location, or event in the definition

---

industrial corporation in 1965, and hence was excluded from the *1966 Plant and Product Directory*.

of their products, would introduce a bias toward increased turnover in these records. The extent of that bias cannot be estimated. Its direction is clear.

Second, these 33 "mergers" by no means account for the total impact of mergers within this group of 494-461 corporations. They are only those mergers in which one of the 494 firms was acquired by another within that group. These are very large corporations. It is therefore unlikely that any merger allowed among them would provide desired market position from the standpoint of the acquiring firm. It is far more likely that it would involve firms in some difficulty with respect to current or anticipated performance. Tables 3-7 and 3-8 are less surprising in this light.

Far more interesting would be the mergers that cannot be identified in the data processed here, but that also probably account for a very substantial portion of the more than 3,500 plants added by these corporations between 1960 and 1965. A major limitation of the *Fortune* data in this context (a context for which the *Fortune* series was not intended) is its failure to identify the source or origin of these acquisitions. In the absence of such identification, no statement can be made regarding the full role of acquisition by merger in the growth and inter-industry activity of these large firms. The only statement that can be made is that those mergers *among* these corporations were accompanied by a high rate of abandonment and product conversion of the plant facilities acquired.

TABLE 3-7:

ENTRY AND EXIT BY PLANTS OF 33 "MERGED" CORPORATIONS,
2-DIGIT INDUSTRY GROUPS, 1960 AND 1965[a]

Industry Code	Total Number of "Merged" Plants 1960	Total Number of "Merged" Plants 1965	Number of Plants Entering	Number of Plants Exiting[b]	
10	3	2	–	1	(1)
11	–	–	–	–	(–)
12	–	–	–	–	(–)
13	3	5	4	2	(2)
14	8	3	–	5	(1)
19	10	5	1	6	(2)
20	112	11	–	101	(–)
21	–	–	–	–	(–)
22	12	12	–	–	(–)
23	2	–	–	2	(–)
24	27	16	–	11	(–)
25	7	4	1	4	(–)
26	8	15	8	1	(1)
27	1	1	1	1	(–)
28	168	104	5	69	(2)
29	15	9	1	7	(3)
30	3	1	–	2	(2)
31	–	–	–	–	(–)
32	22	2	1	21	(1)
33	19	17	3	5	(2)
34	27	16	1	12	(2)
35	52	29	6	29	(4)
36	55	30	2	27	(2)
37	17	15	5	7	(1)
38	14	10	5	9	(2)
39	3	–	–	3	(1)
93	–	–	–	–	(–)
95	–	–	–	–	(–)
99	–	3	3	–	(–)
Total[c]	588	310	47	325	(29)

[a] Includes the plants of 30 corporations disappearing by merger, 1 liquidation and 2 corporations ceasing manufacturing activity.

[b] Exit by "matched" plants shown in parentheses.

[c] Each plant is counted once for each industry group represented.

Source: Same as Table 3-2.

50

TABLE 3-8:

Industry Group	Number of Merged Plants Present 1960	1965	Plants Entering [a]	Plants Exiting Matched	Unmatched
2-digit	588	310	47	29	296
3-digit	671	394	108	51	334
4-digit	724	423	127	70	358

[a] All plants entering are necessarily "matched" plants.
Source: Same as Table 3-2.

Data Processing Appendix

This appendix describes the corporate data from two editions of the *Fortune Plant and Product Directory* upon which much of the analysis reported here is based. The *Plant and Product Directory* should not be confused with the well-known annual *Fortune Directory*. That *Directory* dates from 1954 but contains only financial data, and no product information.

In 1961, for the first time, *Fortune Magazine* produced the *Plant and Product Directory*. That volume, published independently of the magazine and intended primarily for market research purposes, lists all known plants owned or controlled by each of 494 large industrial corporations in 1960. For each plant listed, the location (address), ownership, approximate employment, and 5-digit SIC product classes represented, are provided. The *1961 Fortune Plant and Product Directory* lists 10,181 separate plant facilities.

Cross-tabulated by region (county) and by 5-digit product class, the volume permits ready identification of plants representing potential markets for particular products or services in particular areas. The volume was designed with this use in mind. There was therefore little reason, though for academic purposes it might have been nice, to include the plants of corporations that no longer existed when the volume was published early in 1961. Commonwealth Oil, Union Texas National Gas, and Yuba Consolidated Industries, each among the 500 largest in 1960, were excluded from the *Directory* because of mergers in late 1960 or early 1961. In addition, Amerada Petroleum, City Products, and Superior Oil, also among the 500 largest industrials in 1960, reported no domestic manufacturing facilities, and were excluded from the *1961 Plant and Product Directory* for that reason.

There have been two subsequent editions of the *Directory*. The first, in 1963, closely matched the 1961 version, and lists all known plants of the 500 largest industrials in 1963. The second, the *1966 Plant and Product Directory*, extends the coverage to the 1,000 largest industrial corporations, and lists plant and product information for 16,187 plants owned or controlled by 995 industrials in 1965. Five companies—Commonwealth Oil, International Packers, Superior Oil, Amerada Petroleum, and Getty Oil—among the 1,000 largest, reported no domestic manufacturing activity, and were therefore excluded. Publication of the *Directory* is now discontinued.

All companies among the 494 in the 1961 *Directory* that still continued as active independent corporations in 1965 are included in the 1966 *Directory*. The two directories provide detailed plant information, over a five-year interval, for a very substantial segment of U.S. industry. Short of the confidential records of the Bureau of the Census, and more recently of the Standard and Poor's establishment tapes, no equivalent data set exists.

There are, of course, limitations to these data. The *Fortune Directories* were not compiled with an academic audience in mind. Definitions are less precise, and the plant data less detailed, than would have been desirable for the purpose to which they are put here. The primary source of information for *Fortune* was a mail questionnaire requesting the address, class, and product class of all manufacturing plants operated by the corporation to whom the questionnaire was addressed. The definition of what constituted a plant was left to the respondent. The general presumption was that a distinct location at which manufacturing activity was carried out would be designated as a plant, and that definitions essentially comparable to those of the Bureau of the Census would result. There are instances, however, including inconsistent reporting by Time-Life, Inc. itself, where this can be shown not to have been the case.

The plant data do not include estimates of the output for each individual 5-digit product reported. For multiproduct plants, each 5-digit product is simply listed. Even for single-product plants, the relative importance of the production involved must be estimated from crude employment estimates. Both for 1960 and for 1965, *Fortune* requested identification of plant size only within the following broad categories: fewer than 100 employees, 100 to 499 employees, 500 to 999 employees, 1,000 to 4,999 employees, and more than 5,000 employees. Even this limited information was not obtained in all instances.

Finally, the coverage of the directories is suspect. *Fortune* did not, by any means, rely solely on the response to its mailed questionnaire. Follow-up was by telephone; data supplied were checked wherever possible, corrected and augmented where feasible. The prestige of *Fortune* as the prime business periodical of its type would suggest that a relatively high rate of corporate cooperation would be forthcoming. Nevertheless, no independent check of the completeness of the *Fortune* lists is possible, and there is no guarantee that substantial error is not present. In the processing of data taken from these directories, error of various sorts was identified (and corrected). How much remains is a matter of speculation.

Company and Plant Matching

In the preparation of the data file employed in this study, provision was made for the record of each plant in both 1960 and 1965, and the 1960 and 1965 *Fortune* data were merged to a single record of plant characteristics. One of those characteristics was the ownership of the plant. Thus both plants and companies were matched across the two years.

When two corporations among the 494 in 1960 merged prior to 1965, the corporation created by the merger was considered to be the same corporation (or the successor corporation to) the larger of the two merging firms in terms of assets. A plant owned by a corporation involved in a merger was therefore not considered to have changed its ownership provided it had been owned by the larger of the two merging firms. This procedure was followed regardless of the institutional arrangements surrounding the merger. The larger corporation is the acquiring corporation. The smaller corporation is assumed to have died, and this assumption is carried through to the lists of corporation characteristics provided at the end of this appendix and in the appendices to Chapters IV and V.

The plants of these 494-461 corporations were matched, between 1960 and 1965, by address. The *Fortune* data provided, for each plant, county identification as well as a mailing address. Plants were matched within counties. When a 1960 plant showed the same mailing address as a 1965 plant, the two plants were considered matched—to be the same plant—regardless of the ownership of the plant in either 1960 or 1965. In most counties, the number of plants was relatively small, and the matching process straightforward. In a few counties—for example, Los Angeles, with almost 500 plants listed in 1965—it was difficult. Matching, in the first instance, was carried out by machine. The 1960 and the 1965 plant records were sorted by counties, and plant addresses compared within counties on the basis of the first fifteen alpha-meric characters of the address. If identical in this respect, the plants were considered matched—to be the same plant. Simultaneously, however, a listing was prepared for each county showing the name and address of each machine-matched, and unmatched, plant. This listing was then hand-checked and corrected, with reference to the printed *Fortune Directories,* in a second machine run. This process was repeated three times.

To provide a check on the extent to which this matching process might have been incomplete—primarily because of inadequate address information—the criteria for matching were then changed. *All* "unmatched" plants within each county were matched, irrespective of address, if, between 1960 and 1965, ownership was the same *and* if the same 3-digit SIC code appeared in the listing of the firm's products in 1960 and 1965. This check indicated that only 249 additional plants would be matched by this procedure, and of those the record clearly indicated that different plants were involved, provided that the mailing addresses recorded were at all accurate. Plants do not move from one corner of a county to another. The earlier matching process, despite the high turnover of plant facilities reported earlier in this chapter, appears to have been rather complete.

Of the 494 corporations considered in 1960, the 461 remaining independent manufacturers in 1965 were the Hearst Corporation and the 460 industrials identified in the Appendices to Chapters IV and V. As noted earlier, the full 494, plus Amerada Petroleum, Commonwealth

Oil, International Packers, Superior Oil, Union Texas Natural Gas, and Yuma Consolidated Industries were the 500 largest industrial corporations, as identified by *Fortune*, in 1960.

The 33 disappearances are as follows:

(1) *Acme Steel* and Interlake Iron merged in December 1964 to form Interlake Steel.

(2) *Alco Products* was acquired by the Worthington Corporation in December 1964.

(3) *American Agricultural Chemical* was acquired by Continental Oil in October 1963.

(4) *American Viscose* was acquired by FMC in June 1963.

(5) *Anaconda Wire and Cable* merged with Anaconda in December 1963.

(6) *Baldwin-Lima-Hamilton* was acquired by Armour and Company and merged on July 2, 1965.

(7) *Bell Aerospace* was acquired by Textron in May 1960.

(8) *Boise Cascade* merged with Minnesota and Ontario Paper in January 1965.

(9) *Bridgeport Brass* merged with National Distiller and Chemical in June 1960.

(10) *Champlain Oil and Refining* was acquired by the Celanese Corporation in October 1964.

(11) *Chemstrand* merged with Monsanto in April 1962.

(12) *City Products* ceased manufacturing activity.

(13) *Columbian Carbon* was acquired by Cities Service in January 1962.

(14) *Cosden Petroleum* was acquired by W. R. Grace and Company in January 1960.

(15) *Daystrom* was acquired by Schlumberger in January 1962.

(16) *Delhi-Taylor Oil* was liquidated in 1963.

(17) *Friden* merged with Singer in October 1963.

(18) *Garrett* merged with Signet Oil and Gas in January 1964.

(19) *Ling-Temco Electronics* merged with Chance-Vought in August 1961.

(20) *Litton Industries* merged with Royal McBee in February 1965.

(21) *Martin* merged with American Marietta in October 1961.

(22) *Oliver* was acquired by the White Motor Company in October 1960.

(23) *Pacific Vegetable Oil* ceased manufacturing activity.

(24) *Pepperell Manufacturing* and West Point Manufacturing merged to form West Point Pepperell in March 1965.

(25) *Philco* was acquired by Ford in December 1961.

(26) *Plymouth Oil* was acquired by Marathon Oil in April 1962.

(27) *Pure Oil* was acquired by Union Oil of California in July 1965.

(28) *Siegler* merged with Lear to form Lear-Siegler in June 1962.

(29) *Spencer Kellog* was acquired by Textron in July 1961.

(30) *The Tennessee Corporation* was acquired by Cities Service in June 1963.

(31) *Virginia-Carolina Chemicals* merged with Socony-Mobil Oil in November 1963.

(32) *Yale and Towne Manufacturing* was acquired by Eaton Manufacturing in October 1963.

(33) *W. P. Fuller* merged with Hunt Foods in February 1962.

IV

Corporate Growth, Entry, and Diversification

THE evidence in Chapter III with respect to plant activity gives no key whatsoever to corporate activity. It suggests a good deal of inter-industry fluidity on the part of the plants of the Fortune corporations; it provides no evidence that this behavior is intra-firm, as opposed to inter-firm, as it must be if this inter-industry activity is a corporate rather than a plant phenomenon.

This chapter develops measures of corporate entry and exit and of corporate diversification for these firms, and those measures are in turn related to the growth rates of firms during the 1960 to 1965 period.[1] The purpose is twofold: first, to show the degree to which the *plant* entry and exit documented earlier has led also to *corporate* entry and exit; and, second, to try to isolate a relationship between that kind of inter-industry activity and the growth rate of these large firms. It is not obvious that entry into new industries is generally characteristic of firms that tend to grow rapidly. It is equally plausible that firms that enter new industries may be stimulated to do so by a lack of growth potential within their established markets.

THE SAMPLE

Here the analysis is restricted to 460 corporations for which data, including financial variables, are available

[1] The major findings of this chapter, together with related discussion, appear in Charles H. Berry, "Corporate Growth and

59

for both 1960 and 1965.[2] The 460 are the 461 of the 494 largest in 1960 that survived to 1965, less the Hearst Corporation, a privately held firm for which financial records are not publicly available. The 460 corporations accounted, in 1960, for total assets of $170 billion, about 60 percent of all U.S. corporate industrial assets in that year. By 1965 those assets had increased to a little more than $250 billion, an overall five-year increment of roughly 47 percent.

That growth reflected an increase both in the number of plant facilities and in the number of products reported by these corporations. The number of individual plants reported by the 460 increased from 10,147 in 1960 to 11,589 in 1965. On the average, a firm in this group produced in 3.8, 7.1, and 9.9 separate 2-, 3-, and 4-digit industries, respectively, in 1960. Those averages were 4.4, 8.7, and 13.9 in 1965. Table 4-1 shows the distribution of these 460 corporations by the number of separate industries in which each reported products in 1960 and 1965, and bears out in more detail the increasing diversification of large industrial corporations which has begun to be documented elsewhere.[3] According to these

---

Industrial Diversification," *Journal of Law and Economics*, Vol. xiv (2), October 1971, pp. 371-383.

[2] Data relating to the diversification of these corporations are from the 1961 and 1966 editions of the *Fortune* publication, *Plant and Product Directory*, as outlined in Chapter III and in Chapter III, Appendix. See also the Appendix to this chapter. Total assets for these corporations are as reported in *The Fortune Directory* (Chicago: Time, Inc., 1961) and *The Fortune Directory* (Chicago: Time, Inc., 1966).

[3] See *Economic Report on Corporate Mergers*, Staff Report to the Federal Trade Commission (Government Printing Office, 1969), pp. 219-225. See also Charles H. Berry, "Corporate Bigness and Diversification in Manufacturing," *Ohio State Law Journal*, Vol. 28, No. 3, 1967, pp. 402-426.

data, the average number of 4-digit industries in which products were reported by these firms increased by an astonishing 40 percent between 1960 and 1965.

AN INDEX OF CORPORATE DIVERSIFICATION

The obvious problem is that diversification is to be gauged not only by the number of industries in which a firm is active, but also by the distribution of the firm's productive activity among those industries. A firm, 99 percent of whose sales are accounted for by a single 5-digit product, is scarcely diversified regardless of the number of 4-digit industries represented by the remaining one percent. On the other hand, a firm whose productive activity is

TABLE 4-1:

460 LARGE INDUSTRIAL CORPORATIONS, BY NUMBER OF 2-, 3-, AND 4-DIGIT INDUSTRIES IN WHICH PRODUCTS WERE REPORTED, 1960 AND 1965

Number of Industries	Number of Corporations					
	4-Digit		3-Digit		2-Digit	
	1960	1965	1960	1965	1960	1965
1-5	168	138	217	183	354	310
6-10	136	109	146	126	95	129
11-15	76	87	53	94	11	20
16-20	40	62	28	25	–	1
21-25	16	26	9	18	–	–
26-30	11	12	3	5	–	–
31-35	4	10	1	5	–	–
36-40	3	4	3	1	–	–
41-45	1	4	–	2	–	–
46-50	2	3	–	1	–	–
51-75	3	4	–	–	–	–
76 and over	–	1	–	–	–	–
Total	460	460	460	460	460	460

Source: *Fortune*, Market Research Department, *1961 Plant and Product Directory* (Time, Inc., 1961) and *1966 Plant and Product Directory* (Time, Inc., 1966).

61

equally divided among four 4-digit industries is likely to be "diversified," even though no more than four 5-digit products are involved.

The point is a familiar one, and in the past the most common remedy has been to judge the diversification of a firm either by the ratio of its output in its primary industry to its total output or, alternatively, by the number of industries necessary to account for some fraction—generally 50 percent—of the firm's total production. Gort, for example, uses the former measure, though in addition he introduces the total number of industries represented in the firm's total output.[4]

For the 460 *Fortune* corporations, a more complete index of diversification is here defined as:

$$D = 1 - \sum_{i=1}^{n} p_i^2$$

where p_i is the ratio of the firm's sales in the ith industry to the firm's total sales in n industries. This index is an application of the Herfindahl Summary Index of Industrial Concentration, but applied to the distribution of a firm's industrial activity rather than to the distribution of an industry's sales among firms.[5] Diversification is 0 when a firm is active in a single industry and approaches unity when the firm in question produces equally in a large number of different industries.

[4] See Michael Gort, *Diversification and Integration in American Industry* (Princeton: Princeton University Press, 1960), pp. 9-15.

[5] See Orris C. Herfindahl, "Concentration in the Steel Industry" (Columbia University: Unpublished Ph.D. dissertation, 1950). In the above expression, the "Herfindahl" index has been subtracted from unity to make the index increase with increasing diversification.

This index appears to approximate rather closely what is generally meant by "diversification." It has, in addition, the convenient property that when a firm is equally active in each of several industries, the index of diversification becomes $1 - 1/n$ where n is the number of industries in which the firm is active. For example, a firm producing equally in four industries will yield a diversification index of 1 minus $1/4$, or $3/4$. Any firm with a diversification index of $3/4$, which can be obtained in various ways, is by this measure diversified to a degree equivalent to that of a firm producing equally in 4 industries. This property of the Herfindahl Index has been discussed by Adelman.[6] A few illustrative values of the index are given in Table 4-2.

TABLE 4-2:

ILLUSTRATIVE VALUE OF THE HERFINDAHL-TYPE INDEX OF DIVERSIFICATION

Percent of Firm's Sales in Industry					Index of Diversification
(1)	(2)	(3)	(4)	(5)	
100	–	–	–	–	0
95	5	–	–	–	.10
90	10	–	–	–	.18
80	10	10	–	–	.34
60	40	–	–	–	.48
60	10	10	10	10	.60
50	20	20	10	–	.66
40	20	20	10	10	.74
30	20	20	20	10	.78
20	20	20	20	20	.80

Source: Derived by author. See text for definition of Herfindahl-type Index.

[6] See M. A. Adelman, "Comment on the 'H' Concentration Measure as a Numbers-Equivalent," *Review of Economics and Statistics*, Vol. 51, February 1969, pp. 99-101.

DIVERSIFICATION OF THE FORTUNE CORPORATIONS

Table 4-3 shows the mean values (unweighted) of diversification at the 2-, 3-, and 4-digit levels of the 460 *Fortune* corporations in 1960 and 1965. The 1960 values shown correspond approximately to those that would have been obtained had each of these firms produced equally in 1.6, 2.2, and 2.7, 2-, 3-, and 4-digit industries

TABLE 4-3:

AVERAGE 2-, 3- AND 4-DIGIT DIVERSIFICATION, 460 LARGE
INDUSTRIAL CORPORATIONS, 1960 AND 1965

Level of Diversification	Diversification Index	
	1960	1965
2-digit	.361	.396
3-digit	.548	.586
4-digit	.627	.661

Source: Same as Table 4-1.

respectively. This is very much less diversification—about two-thirds less—than naive extrapolation of the industry counts reported earlier would suggest. Furthermore, the change between 1960 and 1965 is slight—an increase of about 3 percent at the 4-digit level and of 5 percent in terms of 2-digit diversification.[7] Given the initial level of diversification in 1960, that increase, at the 4-digit level, would correspond to what would have occurred with the addition by each firm of about one-tenth of a 4-digit product if the production of each had been divided equally among the 4-digit industries represented. Values

[7] The ranking of these percentages can be misleading. Had a "straight" Herfindahl Index been employed (e.g., $D = \Sigma p_i{}^2$), the ordering of these percentages at the 2- and 4-digit levels would be reversed. The percentages themselves, however, would remain small.

of these indices of diversification are given for each of the 460 corporations in the Appendix to this chapter.

There are two obvious conclusions. First, industry counts for these firms, as shown in Table 4-1 for example, greatly overstate the degree of industrial diversification of these corporations—or at least are highly susceptible to that interpretation. On the average, these corporations were active in 1960 in almost ten 4-digit industries. Production among those industries was sufficiently unequal to make the resulting diversification equivalent, by the measure employed here, to equal production in fewer than three 4-digit industries. The extent of this difference is indicated by Table 4-4, which compares the average

TABLE 4-4:

AVERAGE NUMBER OF INDUSTRIES, AND DIVERSIFICATION
NUMBERS-EQUIVALENT, 460 LARGE INDUSTRIAL
CORPORATIONS, 1960 AND 1965

Industry Level	Number of Industries		Diversification Numbers-Equivalent	
	1960	1965	1960	1965
2-digit	3.8	4.4	1.6	1.7
3-digit	7.1	8.7	2.2	2.4
4-digit	9.9	13.9	2.7	2.9

Source: Same as Table 4-1.

number of industries in which these firms were on the average active with the "Numbers Equivalent" implied by their average level of diversification.[8]

Second, diversification by these firms *did* increase between 1960 and 1965, but not by as much as might have

[8] The "Numbers Equivalent" is defined as the number of industries that would generate the same index of diversification were the production of the firm equally divided among those industries.

65

been expected. While the average number of 4-digit industries in which production was reported by these firms rose by 40 percent between 1960 and 1965, 4-digit diversification, by a measure weighting the relative importance of production within those industries, increased by about 5 percent.[9]

CORPORATE GROWTH AND CHANGING DIVERSIFICATION

These averages, however, take no account of variance in the behavior of individual firms, and substantial decreases as well as increases occurred in the diversification of individual corporations. As a whole, these corporations grew and diversified, but that does not necessarily mean that increasing diversification has been a significant component of relative growth *within* this group of 460. Although what follows suggests that such a relationship is not strong, it also suggests that the relationship is not

[9] Even this is probably an overstatement of changing diversification. The underlying estimates of corporate diversification are, as noted, based on records of each 5-digit product produced within each plant of each company in 1960 and 1965. Production by these plants at the 2-, 3-, and 4-digit levels was estimated by dropping terminal digits, and considering all products of the plant within the same industry category to be the same product. Indices of diversification for the company were prepared by assuming that the output of each multi-product plant was equally divided among the products reported. Each plant was weighted according to its estimated employment. This weighting of products equally within plants, and of plants equally within size categories, would tend to bias upwards the resulting estimates of corporate diversification. If products and plants added between 1960 and 1965 tended to be relatively less important quantitatively than the corresponding average product or plant, change in diversification will also be biased upwards. No check on the quantitative importance of this is possible. See the Appendix to this chapter.

totally in accord with the proposition that increasing diversification is the new route to corporate bigness.

Table 4-5 contains regression results obtained when growth in the assets of these firms between 1960 and

TABLE 4-5:

REGRESSION COEFFICIENTS AND *t*-RATIOS, PERCENT INCREASE IN TOTAL ASSETS ON SELECTED INDEPENDENT VARIABLES, 460 LARGE INDUSTRIAL CORPORATIONS, 1960-1965

Independent Variables	Regression Coefficients and t-Ratios[a]						
	(1)	(2)	(3)	(4)	(5)	(6)	(7)
Total Assets, 1960[b]	-4.23 (-1.56)						
Log_e Total Assets, 1960		-6.98 (-3.31)	-6.35 (-2.99)	-6.48 (-3.06)		-7.11 (-3.38)	-7.06 (-3.29)
Earnings, 1960	1.24 (2.48)	1.29 (2.61)	1.43 (2.88)	1.44 (2.89)	1.18 (2.38)	1.30 (2.63)	1.49 (2.97)
Projected Growth	.345 (2.86)	.375 (3.31)			.337 (2.79)	.374 (3.12)	.374 (3.07)
Percent Change, 4-Digit Diversification	.335 (4.00)	.334 (4.02)	.33 (3.98)	.29 (4.56)	.336 (4.01)	.285 (4.59)	
Percent Change, 2-Digit Diversification	-.113 (-1.04)	-.095 (-.89)	-.10 (-.86)		-.120 (-1.11)		.192 (2.35)
R^2	.08	.10	.08	.08	.08	.10	.07

[a] *t*-Ratios are shown in parentheses.
[b] Defined in dollars X 10^{-5}.

1965 is regressed on independent variables that would be expected to be related to that growth. The regression models are of the usual additive form, unweighted, with intercepts. Corporate growth is defined as the percentage increase in total assets of each corporation between 1960 and 1965. Independent variables are defined as follows:

(1) *Total Assets, 1960*: Total corporate assets in 1960 as reported in *The Fortune Directory* for 1961. Both the raw value and the logarithm of this variable are used, though independently. The variable is included to test for differential growth between the larger and smaller corporations in this sample. That test is appropriate for two reasons. On the one hand, it is often argued that the very large industrial corporation has a great advantage in the growth process, and a good deal of policy attention has been directed to this purely structural aspect of changing industrial organization. On the other hand, it is not unreasonable to suppose the opposite—that a given percentage increase in total assets may, other things being equal, be more readily accomplished by the smaller firm if for no other reason than that the smaller firm is less likely to be constrained by the growth rates of its particular markets. In this context, the variable would make more sense if corporate size were defined in relation to the size of the relevant markets, but that is not attempted here.

(2) *Earnings, 1960*: Net profit after tax as a percent of total assets in 1960, again as reported by the 1961 *Fortune Directory*. This variable is a crude proxy for the availability of internal investment funds. Dividends paid are included on the grounds that the dividend payout ratio is determined internally by the firm. These total earnings are scaled on the same base (total assets) as is the dependent variable. Note that the variable acts not as a rate of return—to which it is clearly related—but as a constraint on internal investment funds available to the firm.

(3) *Projected Growth, 1960-1965*: This variable is defined as $G = \sum_{i=1}^{n} w_i g_i$ where w_i is the proportion of the

68

firm's activity in the ith 4-digit industry, and g_i is the 1958-1963 percentage increase in the value of shipments of that industry. This variable corrects for differential growth among the various 4-digit industries in which these firms are active. The earlier period 1958-1963 is selected on the ground that corporate assets would tend to lag sales.

(4) *Percent Change, 4-Digit Diversification*: Percent change in the Herfindahl Index of diversification at the 4-digit level, 1960-1965.[10]

(5) *Percent Change, 2-Digit Diversification*: As in (4) above, but at the 2-digit level.

In Table 4-5, coefficients on 1960 earnings and on changing 4-digit diversification are consistently positive and significant.[11] If corporate size—total assets in 1960— is entered in logarithms, the coefficient on that variable is also significant, though negative. Within this framework, and for this particular sample, there is no evidence that corporate size has been positively related to corporate growth. What evidence there is suggests the reverse.[12]

The coefficient on the projected growth variable is approximately 0.35. This is substantially (and significantly) below the coefficient of unity that would be consistent with growth by these corporations in exact proportion to

[10] In these regressions, diversification at all levels is measured by a "straight" Herfindahl Index with a negative sign (e.g., $D = -\Sigma p_i^2$). This modification was necessary to permit calculation of percentage change in the 2-digit index, since many firms produce only within a single 2-digit industry group.

[11] Essentially similar results are obtained if changing diversification is measured at the 3- rather than the 4-digit level. The two measures are closely related. Slightly higher t-ratios are obtained with the latter.

[12] The simple correlation between growth and size is also negative; $r = -.12$ with size measured in logarithms.

the growth of their various industries. On the one hand, the significance of the coefficient suggests that the "accident" of initial industrial location *is* a factor explaining some of the relative growth by these firms. On the other, it suggests that such growth has been less rapid than that of the industries or markets in question. In part, this may be a result of the cyclical recovery during the time period considered. In cyclically sensitive industries—steel, for example—growth in sales between 1958 and 1963 probably resulted more in the elimination of excess capacity than in the creation of additional capacity.[13]

Interpretation of the coefficients on the measures of changing diversification is interesting but, given the definition of those variables, not easy. When either variable— changing diversification at the 2- or the 4-digit level— is introduced independently of the other, the coefficient has the expected positive sign and is, by the usual tests, statistically significant. Corporate growth, within this group of 460, is positively associated with increasing diversification, regardless of the level at which that diversification is measured. However, when measures of changing diversification at the 2- and the 4-digit level are introduced simultaneously, that association is positive only at the 4-digit level; and it becomes negative, though not significant, at the 2-digit level. If the signs of the coefficients on those variables are believed—collinearity between the variables does not bias the estimates—this result suggests a rather conventional model of corporate

---

[13] Note that this regression coefficient is equivalent to the product of the inverse of the average initial capital-output ratio and the capital-output ratio of assets added during the five-year period. Since the latter would be expected to be less than the former, the value of that regression coefficient may be a little less surprising than it first appears.

growth: that diversification leading to corporate growth has involved entry to 4-digit industries related to (within the same 2-digit industry group as) those 4-digit industries within which the corporation in question has experienced past success. In other words, the pattern of coefficients obtained is consistent with the thesis that successful (profitable) corporations expand (diversify), but to product areas (industries) related to their areas of past success, and that it is those corporations whose performance and potential growth have been unsatisfactory which are more likely to branch to new and unrelated areas of productive endeavor.[14]

Within this context, Table 4-6 shows similar results employing measures of entry and exit in lieu of the measures of changing diversification in Table 4-5. In these regressions, entry and exit are defined as simple product counts of the number of industries added or dropped at the SIC level indicated. For example, if in 1965 a corporation reported products in two 4-digit industries in which it reported no products in 1960, 4-digit entry for that corporation is two. "Net entry" is defined as the difference between entry and exit and is, therefore, the increase in the number of industries reported between 1960 and 1965.

In Table 4-6, 4-digit entry variables have positive and significant coefficients. The coefficients on 2-digit entry are negative, as in the case of changing diversification at

[14] Note that although the specification of the dependent variable in this regression model would appear to make it susceptible to negative heteroscedacity with respect to the corporate size variable, this turns out not to be true to any substantial degree. The simple correlation between the absolute value of the residual and corporate assets *is* negative, but R^2 is .01 (.04 with corporate assets in log form).

this level although again significance levels are marginal. Although these results are scarcely independent of those of Table 4-5, the somewhat higher level both of overall explanation and of the significance of the 4-digit meas-

TABLE 4-6:

REGRESSION COEFFICIENTS AND *t*-RATIOS, PERCENT INCREASE IN TOTAL ASSETS ON SELECTED INDEPENDENT VARIABLES, 460 LARGE INDUSTRIAL CORPORATIONS, 1960-1965

| Independent Variables | Regression Coefficients and t-Ratios[a] | | | | |
	(1)	(2)	(3)	(4)	(5)
Log_e Total Assets, 1960	-10.09 (4.96)			-9.34 (-4.63)	-10.38 (-5.16)
Earnings, 1960	1.50 (3.21)	1.31 (2.74)	1.24 (2.61)	1.37 (2.94)	1.64 (3.55)
Projected Growth	.235 (2.04)	.203 (1.73)	.232 (1.99)	.275 (2.40)	.215 (1.87)
4-Digit Entry	4.61 (6.83)	4.17 (6.08)			4.19 (6.59)
4-Digit Exit	-1.95 (-1.79)	-2.04 (-1.82)			
4-Digit Net Entry			3.83 (5.89)	4.22 (6.58)	
2-Digit Entry	-4.05 (-1.70)	-3.82 (-1.56)			-3.12 (-1.37)
2-Digit Exit	.559 (.16)	-.340 (-.10)			
2-Digit Net Entry			-2.74 (-1.29)	-3.22 (-1.55)	
R^2	.20	.16	.15	.19	.19

[a]*t*-Ratios are shown in parentheses.

ures is consistent with the interpretation that growth by these corporations has been accompanied by expansion within established 2-digit industry groups, and that the diversification that has accompanied that growth has been more horizontal than conglomerate.

SUMMARY

The results reported in this chapter are based on the growth and diversification of 460 corporations that together account for nearly two-thirds of all U.S. corporate industrial assets. For these firms, the degree both of diversification and of recent change in diversification appears to be considerably less than that which would at first glance be suggested by the number of industries in which these same firms have been active. On the average, the diversification of these firms is about the same as that of a firm with production equally divided among three 4-digit industries concentrated within a single 2-digit industry group. Given that these corporations are large corporations, apt frequently to be vertically integrated, and given also that the Standard Industrial Classification can place vertically related 4-digit industries in different 2-digit industry groups, the degree of diversification indicated by these firms is consistent with a relatively high prevalence of corporate specialization within the group as a whole.

Change in the *average* diversification of these firms is also small relative to the increase in the number of products shown by these firms over the five-year period. At the 4-digit level, the average number of products rose by something like 40 percent; the average index of 4-digit diversification increased by less than four percent. The implication is clear that the products that were added by

73

these firms did not, in general, account for large proportions of their total productive activity.

On the other hand, from a structural standpoint, the addition of the products may be the more significant development. For example, the index of diversification defined earlier could register change simply as a consequence of unintended shifts in market shares within industries without any intent whatsoever on the part of a particular corporation to diversify. Entry, however, necessarily involves a commitment on the part of the corporation to expand or to shift its activities to a new product or set of products. The significance of entry in this context is suggested by the earlier regression results, which show a higher degree of association between corporate growth and the addition of new products than between corporate growth and change in the diversification index.

By far the most interesting aspect of those regression results, however, is related to the nature of the relationship of corporate growth with entry or increasing diversification. The evidence, such as it is, appears to indicate consistently that the 4-digit inter-industry activity that has been most conducive to corporate growth has been *within* rather than *among* 2-digit industry groups. At least one possible interpretation of this finding is that the diversification that has led to relatively rapid rates of corporate growth (or has accompanied it) has not in general been to markets where the entering firm is a new and potentially competitive force. Rather, that "diversification" has been to markets that are related to—and potentially if not actively competitive with—those in which the entering firm will frequently share whatever market power already exists. That kind of diversification is only one small step removed from the consolidation of market power through horizontal acquisition. The issue that is raised by these regression results is far from idle in the context of an increasingly concentrated corporate industrial sector.

The data in this chapter raise this issue. They do not answer it. The measures of the inter-industry activity of these firms—entry and diversification—are not well suited to the purpose of making the kind of distinction that is implied above. More appropriate, though certainly not ideal, would be measures distinguishing for each firm increasing 4-digit diversification (and entry) *within* 2-digit industry groups from that which arises as a consequence of diversification across (or entry to) new 2-digit categories.

Such measures are defined and developed in the following chapter. Chapter V employs these new measures to test the hypothesis that is here suggested: that for these large corporations, growth-related diversification and entry has been within, rather than across, 2-digit industry groups.

Appendix

The indices of corporate diversification reported in this chapter are based on the corporate plant records described in the appendix to Chapter III. Those records provide no direct measure of the output of the plants involved but contain only an indication of approximate plant employment and a listing of 5-digit products.

To obtain the necessary estimates of 2-, 3-, and 4-digit production by SIC categories, the following assumptions were made. All 5-digit products with the same first four digits in the 5-digit code were considered to be the same 4-digit "product." Correspondingly, to obtain 3- and 2-digit classes, the appropriate righthand digits were dropped from the 5-digit code, and identical remaining codes collapsed.

In the case of plants reporting more than one "product" at the level of classification under consideration, the output of the plant was considered to be equally divided among the products reported *at that classification level.* Thus a plant with production in three 4-digit industries in one 2-digit industry group, and in one 4-digit industry within a second 2-digit industry group, would have been considered to have been producing equally within four 4-digit industries but also equally between two 2-digit industry groups. This inconsistency is not present in some alternative indices developed in the following chapter.

Finally, individual plants were weighted according to estimated employment. The weights employed are indicated below.

Employment Class	Plant Weight
Under 100	60
100-499	200
500-999	600
1,000-4,999	1,600
Over 4,999	5,300
Unknown	440

These plant weights approximately correspond to the mean employment of all manufacturing establishments within the employment category shown.

Overall, this procedure assumes that plant production in all industries is proportionate to employment, and that employment within a plant is equal among the different industries represented, regardless of the level at which the industries are classified. Alternative, and intellectually more satisfying, assumptions could have been made—for example, that the output of multi-product plants is divided among products in proportion to total national shipments of those products—but the crudity of the employment data, on which all output estimates *must* be based, did not appear to justify the added expense that would have accompanied more refinement at this stage. Also, the relatively high degree of product specialization of these plants, as reported in Chapter III, mitigates against error in the allocation of within-plant productive activities.

Much more suspect are the plant weights indicated above. As a check of the extent of the error introduced on this account, indices of diversification were calculated employing equal plant weights—that is, weighting each plant equally regardless of its employment class. The simple correlation coefficient between 1960 4-digit diversification with plants *weighted* and 1960 4-digit diversification with plants *unweighted* is .902, suggesting that error in the weights alone ought not to invalidate the measures of diversification for the purpose to which they are put in this chapter.

The following table shows 2- and 4-digit diversification indices for the 460 corporations in 1960 and 1965. The 460 corporations are the 500 largest (in terms of sales) as identified by the 1960 *Fortune Directory of the 500 Largest* (Chicago, Time, Inc., 1961), less those which merged out of existence (or otherwise ceased manufacturing activity) between 1960 and 1965, and less the Hearst Corporation for which financial records are not public. In the case of mergers within this group, the larger of the merging firms was (arbitrarily) considered the successor corporation to the two merging firms. For this reason, the table contains some corporate names that did not exist in 1965. Identification of the corporations is on the basis of the corporate name in 1960.

TABLE 4A-1

COMPANY NAME	DIVERSIFICATION - 1960			DIVERSIFICATION - 1965		
	2-DIGIT	3-DIGIT	4-DIGIT	2-DIGIT	3-DIGIT	4-DIGIT
ACF INDUSTRIES	.7678	.9004	.9005	.7302	.8211	.8211
ABBOTT LABORATORIES	.4976	.5625	.7091	.6639	.7312	.7774
ADDRESSOGRAPH-MULTIGRAPH	.6892	.6901	.8312	.7904	.8269	.8755
ADMIRAL	.3513	.6945	.7118	.5118	.7722	.7998
AIR REDUCTION	.1265	.1327	.1790	.6182	.6570	.7213
ALAN WOOD STEEL	.3765	.4124	.4124	.3576	.3576	.3576
ALLEGHENY LUDLUM STEEL	.4392	.5323	.5323	.4916	.5418	.5422
ALLIED CHEMICAL	.1983	.4567	.8318	.5776	.7746	.8838
ALLIED MILLS	.0	.1444	.1444	.0	.4201	.4201
ALLIS-CHALMERS	.5793	.8394	.8996	.5840	.8561	.9013
ALUMINUM CO. OF AMERICA	.3924	.7583	.8105	.3667	.7531	.7929
AMERICAN BAKERIES	.0	.0195	.1633	.0	.0180	.0705
AMERICAN BOSCH ARMA	.7683	.7942	.7973	.6704	.7483	.7483
AMERICAN BRAKE SHOE	.5497	.6642	.8063	.5439	.6935	.8075
AMERICAN CAN	.5380	.6651	.7767	.5749	.7007	.7635
AMERICAN CHAIN & CABLE	.7946	.8518	.8569	.7955	.8393	.8396
AMERICAN CYANAMID	.4447	.8488	.9174	.4124	.8415	.9212
AMERICAN ENKA	.3088	.6512	.6843	.4907	.7017	.7231
AMERICAN FOREST PRODUCTS	.3991	.7731	.7942	.4516	.7594	.7917
AMERICAN HOME PRODUCTS	.3349	.6321	.8208	.5294	.6675	.8069
AMERICAN MACHINE & FOUNDRY	.8386	.9241	.9455	.8519	.9337	.9407
AMERICAN-MARIETTA	.4785	.5920	.7188	.8433	.8719	.8862
AMERICAN METAL CLIMAX	.6001	.8299	.8918	.7345	.8327	.9268
AMERICAN MOTORS	.2534	.2534	.2534	.2339	.2339	.2371
AMERICAN OPTICAL	.4742	.8555	.8555	.4742	.8559	.8559
AMERICAN PETROFINA	.0	.0	.0	.0	.0	.0
AM. RADIATOR & STD. SANITARY	.7373	.8208	.8881	.7363	.7799	.8907
AMERICAN SMELTING & REFINING	.2026	.6212	.8357	.2929	.6477	.8569
AMERICAN STEEL FOUNDRIES	.6143	.7316	.7837	.6208	.6825	.7252
AMERICAN SUGAR REFINING	.1001	.1007	.1007	.0648	.0652	.3973
AMERICAN TOBACCO	.0	.4300	.4300	.0	.4639	.4639
ANACONDA	.4170	.5706	.7395	.4196	.7000	.8645
ANCHOR HOCKING GLASS	.2526	.4566	.6199	.3714	.5490	.7151
ANDERSON-PRICHARD OIL	.0	.5000	.5000	.0	.0	.0
ANHEUSER-BUSCH	.4576	.7692	.8067	.4537	.7350	.8007
ARCHER-DANIELS-MIDLAND	.5984	.8079	.8500	.6833	.8536	.8774
ARMCO STEEL	.5823	.5827	.7674	.5502	.6559	.6946
ARMOUR	.4834	.6638	.7924	.6752	.7787	.8308
ARMSTRONG CORK	.7696	.8396	.8460	.6823	.8397	.8675
ARMSTRONG RUBBER	.0	.0950	.0950	.0	.0	.0

79

TABLE 4A-1 (CONT.)

COMPANY NAME	DIVERSIFICATION - 1960			DIVERSIFICATION - 1965		
	2-DIGIT	3-DIGIT	4-DIGIT	2-DIGIT	3-DIGIT	4-DIGIT
ASHLAND OIL & REFINING	.0	.3499	.3499	.4839	.6406	.6406
ATLANTIC REFINING	.5000	.6649	.7474	.5000	.6646	.7469
AVCO	.7257	.8598	.8860	.8261	.9038	.9199
AVON PRODUCTS	.0	.0	.0	.3047	.3047	.3047
BABCOCK & WILCOX	.7530	.8346	.8372	.7801	.8844	.8987
BEATRICE FOODS	.0	.3832	.4934	.0441	.5953	.8022
BEAUNIT MILLS	.5499	.7516	.7743	.5569	.8115	.8305
BEECH AIRCRAFT	.5618	.5618	.7778	.4975	.4975	.6652
BEECH-NUT LIFE SAVERS	.C	.5623	.6250	.2596	.7163	.8046
BEMIS BROS. BAG	.5742	.7881	.8087	.7835	.8876	.9281
BENDIX AVIATION	.8238	.9268	.9400	.8199	.9317	.9440
BETHLEHEM STEEL	.7023	.7887	.8974	.6316	.8210	.9056
BIBB MANUFACTURING	.C	.6615	.7370	.0	.6605	.7391
BIGELOW-SANFORD CARPET	.5172	.6963	.7262	.0000	.4206	.6648
BLAW-KNOX	.6263	.8280	.8916	.6825	.8270	.8729
BLISS /E.W./	.4647	.5308	.7480	.7639	.8022	.8670
BOEING AIRPLANE	.3692	.3692	.5465	.4654	.4654	.5816
BORDEN	.1292	.3627	.6075	.3659	.7307	.8300
BORG-WARNER	.7522	.8843	.9233	.7862	.8898	.9227
BOTANY INDUSTRIES	.5255	.7781	.8112	.2596	.3524	.3524
BRIGGS & STRATTON	.6667	.6667	.6667	.6667	.6667	.6667
BRISTOL-MYERS	.0	.4082	.6531	.0641	.5247	.6033
BROWN SHOE	.0530	.2796	.2796	.0966	.2667	.2668
BRUNSWICK-BALKE-COLLENDER	.6519	.6573	.6573	.7674	.7759	.7801
BUCYRUS-ERIE	.C	.0	.1454	.0411	.0411	.2245
BUDD	.7522	.7924	.7981	.6661	.6973	.6973
BURLINGTON INDUSTRIES	.0174	.8316	.8753	.0174	.8279	.8639
BURROUGHS	.2597	.3141	.6005	.1863	.1892	.2013
BUTLER MANUFACTURING	.3582	.3582	.4587	.5326	.6033	.7140
CALIFORNIA PACKING	.0565	.1476	.2961	.0694	.1300	.2701
CALUMET & HECLA	.8075	.8779	.9171	.7158	.8186	.9004
CAMPBELL SOUP	.0	.3750	.7049	.C	.5121	.7690
CAMPBELL TAGGART ASS. BKRIES	.0	.0096	.0096	.0	.0000	.1402
CANADA DRY	.0	.0	.5088	.0	.0	.5164
CANNON MILLS	.C	.5312	.5312	.0	.3576	.3576
CARBORUNDUM	.4882	.5439	.6221	.5550	.6109	.6744
CAREY /PHILIP/ MANUFACTURING	.5685	.5689	.7864	.6135	.6163	.7855
CARNATION	.1423	.6131	.7814	.1617	.6447	.8006
CARRIER	.5413	.6267	.6267	.3126	.4623	.4810
CASE /J.I./	.0090	.5121	.5519	.0	.6057	.6057

TABLE 4A-1 (CONT.)

COMPANY NAME	DIVERSIFICATION - 1960			DIVERSIFICATION - 1965		
	2-DIGIT	3-DIGIT	4-DIGIT	2-DIGIT	3-DIGIT	4-DIGIT
CATERPILLAR TRACTOR	.0	.4225	.4225	.0	.5747	.5747
CECO STEEL PRODUCTS	.0	.0	.4145	.1855	.1855	.5565
CELANESE	.2993	.4518	.6995	.2981	.6567	.7658
CELOTEX	.6466	.6742	.7735	.7767	.8395	.8714
CENTRAL SOYA	.0	.4944	.4944	.0	.4668	.4668
CERRO DE PASCO	.1271	.7138	.7913	.0983	.6273	.7773
CERTAIN-TEED PRODUCTS	.5447	.5691	.5691	.7382	.7868	.7868
CESSNA AIRCRAFT	.3463	.3475	.6675	.4282	.4367	.7391
CHAMPION PAPER & FIBRE	.3970	.7808	.8606	.3052	.7963	.8623
CHAMPION SPARK PLUG	.4800	.4800	.4800	.4800	.4800	.4800
CHANCE VOUGHT AIRCRAFT	.5255	.7094	.7790	.7259	.8295	.8701
CHEMETRON	.6754	.7051	.7445	.2543	.3162	.4164
CHICAGO PNEUMATIC TOOL	.5835	.8360	.8719	.4820	.8147	.8767
CHRYSLER	.4615	.4700	.4701	.4797	.5049	.5049
CINCINNATI MILLING MACHINE	.7578	.8455	.8733	.7656	.8637	.8811
CITIES SERVICE	.1702	.3293	.3293	.6525	.7880	.8264
CLARK EQUIPMENT	.4945	.6053	.7825	.5697	.6976	.8063
CLARK OIL & REFINING	.0	.0	.0	.5000	.5000	.6667
CLEVELAND-CLIFFS IRON	.0	.0	.0	.0	.0	.0
CLEVITE	.6629	.7395	.7395	.7854	.8691	.8770
CLUETT, PEABODY	.2329	.5361	.7360	.0400	.3124	.5358
COCA-COLA	.0	.2180	.3032	.0	.4853	.5188
COLGATE-PALMOLIVE	.0	.2975	.5992	.0	.3200	.6067
COLLINS RADIO	.0	.6409	.6409	.4291	.7146	.7146
COLORADO FUEL & IRON	.6805	.7724	.8288	.7189	.7694	.8162
COLORADO MILLING & ELEVATOR	.0	.0	.2166	.0	.0	.2326
COMBUSTION ENGINEERING	.6400	.7200	.7200	.3698	.6834	.7030
CONE MILLS	.0	.3107	.3107	.1075	.4805	.4805
CONSOLIDATED CIGAR	.0476	.0476	.0476	.1514	.1514	.1514
CONS. ELECTRONICS INDUSTRIES	.2464	.8168	.8446	.4742	.8634	.8737
CONS. WATER POWER & PAPER	.1172	.6504	.6530	.1738	.7031	.7057
CONSOLIDATION COAL	.6488	.6488	.6542	.1895	.1895	.1895
CONSUMERS COOPERATIVE ASSOC.	.7018	.8113	.8622	.5698	.6846	.7500
CONTAINER CORP. OF AMERICA	.3086	.6146	.7819	.2193	.4859	.7615
CONTINENTAL BAKING	.0367	.2022	.2160	.0000	.2136	.2296
CONTINENTAL CAN	.6495	.7686	.8050	.6089	.7444	.7728
CONTINENTAL MOTORS	.5285	.5368	.6164	.5682	.6973	.7572
CONTINENTAL OIL	.2003	.2062	.2080	.5457	.8223	.8586
COPPERWELD STEEL	.0	.3259	.6002	.0	.0644	.6200
CORN PRODUCTS	.0489	.4410	.6897	.0563	.5704	.7433

TABLE 4A-1 (CONT.)

COMPANY NAME	DIVERSIFICATION - 1960			DIVERSIFICATION - 1965		
	2-DIGIT	3-DIGIT	4-DIGIT	2-DIGIT	3-DIGIT	4-DIGIT
CORNING GLASS WORKS	.4419	.4659	.5721	.2712	.3872	.3875
CRANE	.4765	.7456	.8206	.4111	.7201	.7845
CROWN CORK & SEAL	.3018	.5254	.5254	.3047	.6035	.6035
CROWN ZELLERBACH	.0258	.7928	.8456	.3212	.8174	.8473
CRUCIBLE STEEL	.1127	.6528	.7783	.5332	.7405	.8379
CUDAHY PACKING	.3283	.6880	.8025	.1583	.7118	.7950
CUMMINS ENGINE	.0	.0899	.0899	.1509	.4519	.4519
CURTIS PUBLISHING	.5000	.6176	.6176	.5000	.5937	.5937
CURTISS-WRIGHT	.7257	.8072	.8970	.7268	.8211	.9061
CUTLER-HAMMER	.4910	.7952	.8285	.2983	.7703	.7728
DAN RIVER MILLS	.0	.7368	.7481	.0	.7871	.7871
DANA	.6054	.6822	.6924	.6962	.8310	.8329
DAYCO	.6250	.8122	.8311	.6858	.7843	.7924
DEERE	.2113	.5188	.5328	.1740	.4962	.5108
DETROIT STEEL	.1068	.1068	.1068	.0	.0	.0
DI GIORGIO FRUIT	.2975	.7180	.8260	.2571	.5941	.8237
DIAMOND ALKALI	.1191	.5184	.7876	.5298	.7247	.8644
DIAMOND NATIONAL	.7336	.8602	.8865	.8130	.8864	.9052
DOLE	.4628	.6171	.6942	.4170	.6270	.7546
DONNELLEY /R.R./ & SONS	.0	.4592	.5952	.0	.4592	.5952
DOUGLAS AIRCRAFT	.2960	.2960	.6064	.3445	.3445	.7186
DOW CHEMICAL	.3449	.6520	.8924	.8189	.9200	.9527
DRESSER INDUSTRIES	.6111	.8368	.8607	.6840	.8731	.9105
DU PONT /E.I./ DE NEMOURS	.2953	.7788	.9128	.3355	.7808	.9103
EAGLE-PICHER	.8646	.8994	.9271	.8849	.9356	.9510
EASTERN GAS & FUEL ASSOCIATES	.0	.0	.0	.0	.0	.0
EASTERN STATES FARMERS EXCH.	.4986	.4986	.5983	.4470	.6968	.7627
EASTMAN KODAK	.6111	.8380	.8495	.5417	.8333	.8426
EATON MANUFACTURING	.6033	.6534	.6563	.7230	.8500	.8628
EKCO PRODUCTS	.3665	.7194	.8386	.5900	.8595	.8972
ELECTRIC AUTOLITE	.6600	.8134	.8876	.8120	.8656	.8946
ELECTRIC STORAGE BATTERY	.2256	.4868	.5732	.2718	.4588	.5862
EMERSON ELEC. MANUFACTURING	.7293	.8618	.8824	.6149	.8156	.8393
ENDICOTT JOHNSON	.2671	.4785	.5184	.2604	.2604	.2604
ENGELHARD INDUSTRIES	.7593	.8698	.8721	.7842	.8881	.8881
EVANS PRODUCTS	.7323	.8300	.8379	.5669	.6819	.8461
EX-CELL-O	.4452	.7664	.8531	.5673	.7475	.8479
FAIRBANKS WHITNEY	.6741	.8945	.9045	.7892	.8939	.9038
FAIRCHILD ENGINE & AIRPLANE	.6507	.6758	.7733	.2115	.2257	.5403
FAIRMONT FOODS	.0	.1732	.6091	.0	.5116	.7178

82

TABLE 4A-1 (CONT.)

COMPANY NAME	DIVERSIFICATION - 1960			DIVERSIFICATION - 1965		
	2-DIGIT	3-DIGIT	4-DIGIT	2-DIGIT	3-DIGIT	4-DIGIT
FALSTAFF BREWING	.0	.0	.0	.0	.0	.1420
FEDERAL-MOGUL-BOWER BEARINGS	.5319	.5488	.7101	.6934	.7923	.8547
FEDERAL PAPER BOARD	.4215	.6532	.6825	.4824	.6581	.6849
FIBREBOARD PAPER PRODUCTS	.4243	.7481	.8687	.4947	.7551	.8484
FIRESTONE TIRE & RUBBER	.7895	.9062	.9223	.6816	.8488	.8597
FLINTKOTE	.7135	.8919	.9258	.6209	.8721	.9244
FOOD MACHINERY & CHEMICAL	.7121	.8264	.9091	.7165	.8743	.9374
FORD MOTOR	.5866	.6168	.6180	.6033	.6216	.6226
FOREMOST DAIRIES	.0293	.4932	.6811	.0000	.4352	.6748
FOSTER WHEELER	.4787	.5654	.6087	.2778	.2778	.3044
FRUEHAUF TRAILER	.0861	.0861	.0861	.0938	.6091	.6117
GARDNER-DENVER	.1197	.7708	.8476	.1101	.7505	.8654
GENERAL AMER. TRANSPORTATION	.7636	.8427	.8549	.7387	.8067	.8349
GENERAL ANILINE & FILM	.6555	.8047	.8469	.6602	.8153	.8603
GENERAL BAKING	.0	.0	.0	.0	.0	.2083
GENERAL CABLE	.3824	.3941	.3952	.4388	.4483	.4525
GENERAL DYNAMICS	.7924	.8053	.8253	.8648	.8879	.9166
GENERAL ELECTRIC	.5898	.9211	.9530	.6214	.9325	.9640
GENERAL FOODS	.1982	.7904	.8458	.2735	.7752	.8486
GENERAL MILLS	.4522	.6126	.8414	.2674	.6419	.8295
GENERAL MOTORS	.6915	.7784	.7870	.6674	.7543	.7739
GENERAL PRECISION EQUIPMENT	.7285	.8950	.9199	.7406	.8784	.9147
GEN. TELEPHONE & ELECTRONICS	.3849	.8132	.9166	.4507	.8527	.9260
GENERAL TIRE & RUBBER	.7553	.8521	.8618	.7401	.8124	.9044
GENESCO	.5362	.6676	.6817	.5670	.8039	.8556
GEORGIA-PACIFIC	.0600	.5286	.5286	.6215	.8782	.9142
GERBER PRODUCTS	.4473	.8061	.8061	.2692	.7796	.7796
GILLETTE	.5417	.5417	.5417	.5142	.5142	.5142
GLEN ALDEN	.4200	.5400	.5400	.4628	.6281	.6281
GLIDDEN	.3705	.7021	.7306	.4881	.8089	.8353
GOODRICH /B.F./	.5860	.8210	.8242	.5857	.8353	.8398
GOODYEAR TIRE & RUBBER	.6815	.8000	.8164	.7042	.8369	.8449
GRACE /W.R./	.4974	.8243	.8867	.7105	.8928	.9126
GRANITE CITY STEEL	.5000	.5000	.5000	.5000	.5000	.5000
GREAT WESTERN SUGAR	.0	.0	.0	.0997	.0997	.C997
GRINNELL	.2201	.2851	.6020	.5351	.6014	.7689
GRUMMAN AIRCRAFT ENGINEERING	.5171	.6895	.6966	.5007	.7155	.7155
GULF OIL	.0	.0	.0	.4010	.4628	.4864
HANDY & HARMAN	.0	.6665	.6665	.0	.6627	.6627
HANNA MINING	.3403	.4338	.4338	.2815	.3608	.3608

83

TABLE 4A-1 (CONT.)

COMPANY NAME	DIVERSIFICATION - 1960			DIVERSIFICATION - 1965		
	2-DIGIT	3-DIGIT	4-DIGIT	2-DIGIT	3-DIGIT	4-DIGIT
HARBISON-WALKER REFRACTORIES	.0	.4999	.5697	.0	.4583	.6136
HARNISCHFEGER	.5260	.5882	.7053	.2406	.2406	.6007
HARSCO	.7026	.8205	.8754	.7382	.8620	.9005
HART SCHAFFNER & MARX	.2436	.7089	.7589	.0000	.6667	.7500
HEINZ /H.J./	.0	.5347	.7771	.0	.5810	.7857
HERCULES POWDER	.3583	.7316	.8224	.3154	.7686	.8694
HERSHEY CHOCOLATE	.0	.0	.0	.0	.0	.1800
HOOKER CHEMICAL	.1069	.5618	.7646	.3779	.6589	.8430
HORMEL /GEORGE A./	.0	.0	.2812	.0	.0	.4864
HOUDAILLE INDUSTRIES	.8342	.8898	.9036	.8443	.8923	.9135
HOWE SOUND	.6746	.8764	.8951	.5643	.8405	.8783
HUMBLE OIL & REFINING	.4528	.4528	.4528	.4132	.4479	.4562
HUNT FOODS & INDUSTRIES	.5357	.7482	.8552	.5178	.7559	.8633
HUPP	.6506	.7634	.8208	.7447	.8457	.9011
HYGRADE FOOD PRODUCTS	.0	.3169	.5752	.0	.3730	.6142
I-T-E CIRCIUT BREAKER	.4561	.6343	.6638	.5995	.7037	.7323
IDEAL CEMENT	.0609	.0968	.1167	.0	.0349	.0349
INGERSOLL-RAND	.3704	.8148	.8571	.2778	.8185	.8642
INLAND CONTAINER	.0	.0	.0	.0	.0	.0
INLAND STEEL	.4611	.5210	.7517	.4687	.5347	.7722
INTERCHEMICAL	.3547	.6505	.7556	.3307	.6592	.7720
INTERLAKE IRON	.0	.0	.0	.6292	.6775	.7157
INTERNAT. BUSINESS MACHINES	.5373	.5373	.5539	.4783	.4990	.5108
INTERNATIONAL HARVESTER	.5700	.8237	.8327	.6431	.7904	.7950
INTERNAT. MINERALS & CHEMICAL	.5606	.7134	.8390	.3969	.5609	.5768
INTERNATIONAL PAPER	.3679	.8166	.8361	.2207	.7560	.7882
INTERNATIONAL SHOE	.0947	.2782	.3242	.0983	.2709	.3037
INTERNATIONAL TEL. & TEL.	.1956	.3897	.5081	.5629	.8066	.8361
INTERSTATE BAKERIES	.0	.0	.0	.0	.0	.0
ISLAND CREEK COAL	.0	.0	.0	.0	.0	.0
JOHNS-MANVILLE	.6538	.6686	.8561	.7686	.7955	.8976
JOHNSON & JOHNSON	.6941	.7681	.7988	.7572	.8128	.8366
JONES & LAUGHLIN STEEL	.1850	.5145	.7526	.1634	.4892	.6951
JOSLYN MJF. & SUPPL	.7239	.7821	.8661	.7735	.8259	.8719
JOY MANUFACTURING	.0403	.4754	.7746	.0688	.4963	.7986
KAISER ALUMINUM & CHEMICAL	.4908	.7346	.8171	.4261	.7055	.7827
KAISER INDUSTRIES	.2719	.4787	.4788	.2367	.2879	.3882
KAISER STEEL	.4638	.7186	.7425	.4462	.7148	.7354
KAYSER-ROTH	.5224	.7517	.8561	.5179	.7381	.8916
KELLOGG	.0	.0441	.4511	.0	.0	.4628

84

TABLE 4A-1 (CONT.)

COMPANY NAME	DIVERSIFICATION - 1960			DIVERSIFICATION - 1965		
	2-DIGIT	3-DIGIT	4-DIGIT	2-DIGIT	3-DIGIT	4-DIGIT
KELSEY-HAYES	.6114	.8002	.8296	.5402	.7433	.7733
KENDALL	.6313	.8325	.8413	.6163	.8511	.8591
KENNECOTT COPPER	.0519	.5557	.7198	.0	.6146	.7094
KERR-MCGEE OIL INDUSTRIES	.6327	.6928	.7129	.7092	.7531	.7831
KEYSTONE STEEL & WIRE	.3920	.5123	.5462	.3955	.5146	.5510
KIMBERLY-CLARK	.4217	.7045	.7399	.3941	.7344	.7655
KOPPERS	.6647	.7431	.7577	.8125	.8960	.9093
KROEHLER MANUFACTURING	.2132	.2132	.4924	.1801	.2879	.4703
LACLEDE STEEL	.3084	.3084	.6349	.4928	.4928	.6379
LEAR	.7315	.8611	.8948	.7238	.8930	.9019
LEHIGH PORTLAND CEMENT	.0	.0	.0	.0	.0476	.0476
LEVER BROTHERS	.4616	.4840	.6123	.4626	.4626	.5914
LIBBEY-OWENS-FORD GLASS	.0	.0253	.0253	.0	.0247	.0247
LIBBY, MCNEILL & LIBBY	.0424	.1438	.6901	.0948	.1306	.4568
LIGGETT & MYERS TOBACCO	.0	.4152	.4152	.0997	.4986	.4986
LILLY /ELI/	.1247	.1247	.7073	.2027	.2027	.7249
LILY TULIP CUP	.1207	.2331	.2331	.1673	.2449	.2449
LINK-BELT	.2349	.6275	.7946	.1567	.5993	.7964
LIPTON /THOMAS J./	.0	.3275	.3427	.0	.5571	.6720
LOCKHEED AIRCRAFT	.7819	.8003	.8085	.6596	.7011	.7632
LONE STAR CEMENT	.0	.0	.0	.0	.0	.0
LONE STAR STEEL	.3200	.6400	.6400	.0	.5000	.5000
LORILLARD /P./	.0	.3750	.3750	.0	.5000	.5000
LOWENSTEIN /M./ & SONS	.1244	.5379	.5557	.1372	.5547	.5766
LUKENS STEEL	.6667	.6667	.6667	.6667	.6667	.6667
MACK TRUCKS	.0	.0	.0	.0	.0	.0
MAGNAVOX	.4170	.6975	.6975	.6486	.7838	.7838
MALLORY /P.R./	.4387	.8234	.8250	.1554	.6107	.6163
MASONITE	.0220	.0220	.0220	.4179	.4179	.4179
MAYER /OSCAR/	.0796	.0796	.5369	.0666	.0666	.5232
MAYTAG	.0	.0	.0	.0	.0	.0
MCCALL	.4993	.5348	.5348	.4498	.7170	.7877
MCDONNELL AIRCRAFT	.7500	.8333	.8750	.7500	.8000	.8333
MCGRAW-EDISON	.5729	.8291	.9059	.5923	.8386	.9127
MCGRAW-HILL PUBLISHING	.0	.6667	.6667	.0	.6667	.6667
MCLOUTH STEEL	.0	.0	.0	.0	.0	.0
MEAD	.1150	.8086	.8464	.1953	.8298	.8759
MERCK	.3482	.5335	.8009	.0130	.4477	.7873
MERITT-CHAPMAN & SCOTT	.7657	.8044	.8513	.5985	.5987	.7308
MIDLAND-ROSS	.5751	.7070	.8439	.7552	.8653	.9111

TABLE 4A-1 (CONT.)

COMPANY NAME	DIVERSIFICATION - 1960			DIVERSIFICATION - 1965		
	2-DIGIT	3-DIGIT	4-DIGIT	2-DIGIT	3-DIGIT	4-DIGIT
MILES LABORATORIES	.0	.0792	.2192	.2137	.3762	.4861
MINNEAPOLIS-HONEYWELL REG.	.6786	.8502	.8877	.7305	.8599	.8910
MINNESOTA MINING & MFG.	.8626	.9392	.9482	.8582	.9183	.9346
MINNESOTA & ONTARIO PAPER	.0697	.5348	.5348	.4319	.8615	.8821
MOHASCO INDUSTRIES	.0	.5600	.7589	.6077	.7414	.8136
MONSANTO CHEMICAL	.0339	.8253	.8517	.5699	.8181	.8663
MORRELL /JOHN/	.0	.3546	.5721	.0	.3367	.5182
MOTOROLA	.3853	.6641	.6641	.1723	.7193	.7193
NATIONAL BISCUIT	.0985	.2701	.4846	.0960	.3855	.5605
NATIONAL CAN	.0	.0	.0	.0333	.0333	.0333
NATIONAL CASH REGISTER	.6763	.6763	.6797	.6883	.6914	.7513
NATIONAL DAIRY PRODUCTS	.0587	.5248	.7626	.0838	.6073	.7436
NATIONAL DISTILLERS & CHEM	.6589	.6906	.7019	.7462	.8165	.8339
NATIONAL GYPSUM	.3032	.7877	.8117	.3562	.7992	.8173
NATIONAL HOMES	.0987	.0987	.0987	.1494	.1930	.1930
NATIONAL LEAD	.6468	.8578	.8987	.6337	.8467	.8934
NATIONAL STEEL	.1244	.1254	.1276	.0855	.0855	.0869
NATIONAL SUGAR REFINING	.0	.0	.0	.0	.0	.0
NEW YORK TIMES	.0	.0	.0	.0	.0	.0
NEWPORT NEWS SHIPBUILDING	.5000	.5000	.5000	.5000	.5000	.5000
NORTH AMERICAN AVIATION	.6099	.6375	.8129	.8083	.8174	.8611
NORTHROP	.7294	.7455	.7884	.7115	.7663	.8657
NORTHWESTERN STEEL & WIRE	.0	.0	.5000	.0	.0	.5000
NORTON	.7917	.8056	.8148	.7765	.8726	.9210
OHIO OIL	.4200	.4200	.4200	.5157	.5157	.5157
OLIN MATHIESON CHEMICAL	.6473	.8873	.9473	.7252	.9142	.9556
OTIS ELEVATOR	.0	.0	.0	.0	.0	.0
OUTBOARD MARINE	.1913	.2583	.2583	.6122	.8229	.8229
OWENS-CORNING FIBERGLAS	.3794	.6498	.6498	.3877	.6566	.6566
OWENS-ILLINOIS GLASS	.5025	.6387	.7184	.4764	.5438	.6807
OXFORD PAPER	.3750	.3750	.3750	.0	.0	.0
PABST BREWING	.0465	.0918	.3235	.0605	.1191	.2780
PACIFIC CAR & FOUNDRY	.5812	.8016	.8677	.5606	.7818	.8615
PARKE, DAVIS	.2778	.6111	.7326	.1653	.5620	.7810
PEABODY COAL	.0	.0	.0	.0	.0	.0
PENNSALT CHEMICALS	.2615	.7710	.8914	.5447	.7975	.9059
PEPSI-COLA	.0	.0581	.1424	.0	.0	.0000
PERMANENTE CEMENT	.1995	.6383	.6686	.3682	.7291	.7292
PET MILK	.0	.5645	.6694	.0	.7317	.8138
PFIZER /CHAS./	.1434	.5667	.7254	.2862	.5421	.7937

Growth, Entry, and Diversification

TABLE 4A-1 (CONT.)

COMPANY NAME	DIVERSIFICATION - 1960			DIVERSIFICATION - 1965		
	2-DIGIT	3-DIGIT	4-DIGIT	2-DIGIT	3-DIGIT	4-DIGIT
PHELPS DODGE	.1571	.5697	.6492	.2544	.6214	.6880
PHILADELPHIA & READING	.5957	.6297	.8528	.7351	.7954	.8719
PHILIP MORRIS	.6166	.7560	.7889	.6744	.7385	.7392
PHILLIPS PETROLEUM	.4403	.6071	.6280	.7625	.8049	.8105
PILLSBURY	.0331	.2699	.6361	.0322	.2201	.6356
PITTSBURGH PLATE GLASS	.5383	.7163	.7294	.3907	.6932	.7001
PITTSBURGH STEEL	.0	.1255	.5942	.3095	.4153	.6652
POLAROID	.0	.5000	.5000	.0	.5000	.5000
PORTER /H.K./	.8392	.9330	.9544	.8263	.9266	.9500
POTLATCH FORESTS	.4305	.8522	.9034	.4988	.7973	.8135
PROCTER & GAMBLE	.6364	.7330	.7976	.6303	.7496	.8392
PULLMAN	.2303	.5954	.5954	.1797	.5830	.5830
QUAKER OATS	.2673	.4130	.7441	.2169	.6674	.7809
RADIO CORP. OF AMERICA	.3276	.6904	.8710	.4598	.7663	.8884
RALSTON PURINA	.0225	.3050	.4175	.1908	.6325	.6799
RATH PACKING	.0	.0	.3365	.0	.0	.4600
RAYBESTOS-MANHATTAN	.6764	.7234	.8222	.5371	.5840	.6867
RAYONIER	.0	.3047	.3047	.0	.3047	.3047
RAYTHEON	.4601	.6813	.7946	.5411	.7858	.8375
REICHHOLD CHEMICALS	.2433	.6085	.7404	.2067	.5520	.6336
RELIANCE ELECTRIC & ENGNG	.3107	.3107	.3698	.4444	.4444	.6111
REMINGTON ARMS	.4234	.5633	.5646	.5366	.7462	.7476
REPUBLIC AVIATION	.6737	.7607	.8063	.6551	.7423	.8098
REPUBLIC STEEL	.1568	.2615	.4161	.3382	.3527	.4918
REVERE COPPER & BRASS	.2281	.3116	.5637	.5013	.5720	.6884
REVLON	.1200	.1890	.2959	.4390	.4622	.5473
REXALL DRUG & CHEMICAL	.5440	.7017	.7027	.5761	.6356	.6412
REYNOLDS METALS	.6223	.8089	.8244	.5595	.7760	.7885
REYNOLDS /R.J./ TOBACCO	.0	.5000	.5000	.6644	.8209	.8247
RHEEM MANUFACTURING	.5565	.7571	.7968	.5834	.8438	.8765
RICHFIELD OIL	.0	.0	.0	.0	.0	.0
RIEGEL TEXTILE	.4972	.6460	.6503	.0651	.1286	.1288
ROBERTSHAW-FULTON CONTROLS	.6341	.7026	.7157	.5589	.7156	.7191
ROCKWELL MANUFACTURING	.7566	.7943	.8102	.7692	.8202	.8405
ROCKWELL-STANDARD	.5811	.6916	.7004	.4932	.6761	.6809
ROHM & HAAS	.0	.6763	.7609	.0799	.7475	.8119
ROHR AIRCRAFT	.4989	.4989	.4989	.4625	.4625	.4625
ROYAL MCBEE	.4071	.4175	.6649	.8029	.9186	.9427
RUBEROID	.7305	.7661	.8487	.6670	.6871	.8013
RYAN AERONAUTICAL	.6288	.6555	.7200	.6150	.6150	.7950

87

TABLE 4A-1 (CONT.)

COMPANY NAME	DIVERSIFICATION - 1960			DIVERSIFICATION - 1965		
	2-DIGIT	3-DIGIT	4-DIGIT	2-DIGIT	3-DIGIT	4-DIGIT
ST. JOSEPH LEAD	.6235	.6235	.7731	.6193	.7459	.8562
ST. REGIS PAPER	.3961	.8280	.8838	.3053	.8043	.8888
SCHENLEY INDUSTRIES	.2528	.2537	.5061	.2611	.2611	.4924
SCHERING	.0	.1800	.3400	.0	.0673	.5379
SCOTT PAPER	.0814	.6228	.6876	.0220	.5998	.7278
SCOVILL MANUFACTURING	.8342	.8965	.9056	.8304	.8825	.9032
SEABOARD ALLIED MILLING	.0	.5926	.5926	.0	.4617	.4617
SEAGRAM /JOSEPH E./ & SONS	.1818	.5893	.5893	.2277	.2325	.2325
SHARON STEEL	.0360	.0360	.0883	.2610	.2627	.3584
SHELL OIL	.5747	.6157	.6683	.6167	.6931	.7114
SHERWIN-WILLIAMS	.4066	.6617	.7126	.4038	.7353	.7981
SIGNAL OIL & GAS	.6088	.7376	.7376	.5506	.6033	.7837
SIMMONS	.0	.3177	.7192	.2995	.5773	.7316
SINCLAIR OIL	.6164	.7353	.7410	.6623	.7881	.8248
SINGER MANUFACTURING	.6879	.7455	.7827	.6912	.8672	.9112
SKELLY OIL	.4512	.4512	.4512	.5391	.5391	.5625
SMITH /A.O./	.7930	.8758	.8911	.7787	.8214	.8490
SMITH-CORONA MARCHANT	.5683	.5683	.6963	.2228	.2228	.5557
SMITH KLINE & FRENCH LABS.	.3378	.3467	.4933	.3218	.3876	.4280
SOCONY MOBILE OIL	.0789	.0797	.0797	.6495	.6832	.6974
SOUTHERN STATES COOPERATIVE	.4970	.6302	.6302	.4962	.4962	.4962
SPERRY RAND	.7306	.8758	.8911	.7450	.8666	.8850
SPRINGS COTTON MILLS	.2238	.3788	.3788	.2225	.5932	.5932
SQUARE D	.0	.4705	.5376	.0	.5253	.5627
STALEY /A.E./ MANUFACTURING	.2822	.6332	.6332	.2822	.6369	.6369
STANDARD BRANDS	.3127	.8089	.8403	.2580	.8081	.8640
STANDARD KOLLSMAN	.5283	.7793	.7803	.6428	.8516	.8516
STANDARD OIL OF CALIFORNIA	.4745	.6548	.6648	.4620	.6152	.6239
STANDARD OIL /IND./	.0273	.0331	.0331	.4266	.5254	.5334
STANDARD OIL /OHIO/	.2206	.2206	.2281	.4636	.4636	.5291
STANDARD PACKAGING	.5782	.8694	.9187	.6616	.8842	.9441
STANDARD PRESSED STEEL	.5059	.6162	.6336	.4545	.5518	.5518
STANLEY WORKS	.3671	.5988	.7663	.5199	.7879	.8408
STAUFFER CHEMICAL	.2868	.5191	.7773	.2516	.5383	.7856
STERLING DRUG	.1932	.5648	.7480	.0332	.4741	.7205
STEVENS /J.P./	.0	.6290	.6290	.0303	.6920	.6937
STEWART-WARNER	.8497	.9258	.9431	.8279	.9343	.9428
STOKELY-VAN CAMP	.0	.0998	.5507	.1657	.2707	.6068
STUDEBAKER-PACKARD	.7468	.8045	.8093	.5559	.7724	.8152
SUN OIL	.3750	.3750	.3750	.5000	.5000	.5000

TABLE 4A-1 (CONT.)

COMPANY NAME	DIVERSIFICATION - 1960			DIVERSIFICATION - 1965		
	2-DIGIT	3-DIGIT	4-DIGIT	2-DIGIT	3-DIGIT	4-DIGIT
SUNBEAM	.6763	.8419	.8419	.6690	.7232	.7232
SUNDSTRAND	.3151	.4368	.4412	.3628	.3934	.4087
SUNRAY MID-CONTINENT OIL	.5000	.5000	.5000	.0	.0	.0
SUNSHINE BISCUITS	.0	.5001	.5008	.0	.5237	.5243
SWIFT	.2801	.5075	.6317	.2611	.4656	.6053
TAPPAN	.1420	.1420	.3284	.5233	.5233	.6653
TECUMSEH PRODUCTS	.2975	.6322	.6322	.3161	.6499	.6499
TEXACO	.0	.5562	.5562	.2604	.4933	.4933
TEXAS INSTRUMENTS	.7195	.8416	.8570	.7391	.8846	.8889
TEXTRON	.8277	.9213	.9284	.8887	.9552	.9656
THIOKOL CHEMICAL	.2314	.2369	.6084	.4582	.4726	.5092
THOMPSON RAMO WOOLDRIDGE	.7587	.8990	.9088	.8012	.9104	.9155
TIDEWATER OIL	.4987	.4987	.5878	.5000	.5000	.5992
TIME INC.	.4644	.7914	.8586	.4753	.8148	.8395
TIMES-MIRROR	.3688	.5400	.5532	.3390	.7922	.8121
TIMKEN ROLLER BEARING	.4561	.4869	.4869	.3023	.3350	.3350
TOBIN PACKING	.0	.0	.0517	.0	.0	.1528
TODD SHIPYARDS	.8092	.8671	.8904	.8195	.8808	.9044
TRANE	.6447	.7622	.7639	.5954	.6950	.6950
TUNG-SOL ELECTRIC	.2504	.4616	.6564	.3200	.7050	.7417
UNDERWOOD	.1975	.1975	.5926	.2037	.2037	.5988
UNION BAG-CAMP PAPER	.4572	.8096	.8326	.1157	.8035	.8348
UNION CARBIDE	.7707	.8794	.8985	.7546	.8595	.9288
UNION OIL OF CALIFORNIA	.4922	.4922	.4922	.4058	.4058	.4058
UNION TANK CAR	.6671	.7619	.7619	.6618	.7401	.7401
UNITED AIRCRAFT	.3751	.3872	.7062	.2504	.2640	.6604
UNITED BISCUIT	.0	.0	.0	.0	.0997	.0997
UNITED MERCHANTS & MFRS.	.0340	.4277	.4277	.0340	.4277	.4277
UNITED SHOE MACHINERY	.8179	.8898	.8965	.7473	.8762	.8877
U. S. GYPSUM	.4356	.6076	.6583	.5620	.6933	.7418
U. S. INDUSTRIES	.3913	.6336	.8677	.5635	.6659	.7392
U. S. PIPE & FOUNDRY	.0903	.4646	.5582	.0958	.3342	.4384
U. S. PLYWOOD	.1381	.5456	.6597	.1263	.5998	.6275
U. S. RUBBER	.3790	.7855	.7858	.5698	.8434	.8467
U. S. STEEL	.6825	.8003	.8867	.6846	.8040	.8845
UNIVERSAL-CYCLOPS STEEL	.5045	.6862	.7280	.5429	.8012	.8253
UNIVERSAL MATCH	.7991	.8839	.9055	.7553	.8613	.8879
UPJOHN	.0	.5000	.5000	.0868	.6983	.7989
VICK CHEMICAL	.2604	.4734	.6923	.4600	.6778	.7970
VULCAN MATERIALS	.5830	.7624	.8624	.6238	.7249	.8622

89

TABLE 4A-1 (CONT.)

COMPANY NAME	DIVERSIFICATION - 1960			DIVERSIFICATION - 1965		
	2-DIGIT	3-DIGIT	4-DIGIT	2-DIGIT	3-DIGIT	4-DIGIT
WAGNER ELECTRIC	.5249	.6791	.6791	.5090	.6787	.6787
WALWORTH	.1528	.1528	.2485	.1244	.1244	.1244
WARD BAKING	.0	.0789	.0789	.0	.1810	.3333
WARNER-LAMBERT PHARM.	.7533	.8247	.8505	.5392	.7249	.8389
WEST POINT MANUFACTURING	.0	.5255	.5301	.0985	.6113	.6142
WEST VIRGINIA PULP & PAPER	.2563	.7540	.7658	.3550	.7761	.8152
WESTERN ELECTRIC	.4604	.5692	.7485	.3427	.5397	.6766
WESTERN PRINTING & LITH.	.0208	.7613	.8599	.0000	.7595	.8596
WESTINGHOUSE AIR BRAKE	.5192	.7042	.8192	.6763	.8100	.8289
WESTINGHOUSE ELECTRIC	.6746	.9361	.9674	.6662	.9349	.9674
WEYERHAEUSER	.4961	.8109	.8700	.5266	.8421	.8768
WHEELING STEEL	.1876	.1876	.4158	.3267	.3543	.4643
WHIRLPOOL	.4986	.4986	.7924	.5054	.5054	.7999
WHITE MOTOR	.2187	.2292	.2648	.6054	.7335	.7520
WILSON	.4525	.5251	.5824	.4832	.5198	.6498
WORTHINGTON	.5207	.8108	.8565	.6568	.8654	.8899
WRIGLEY /WM./ JR.	.0	.0	.0	.0	.0	.0
WYANDOTTE CHEMICALS	.6985	.7771	.8849	.6802	.7672	.8826
YOUNGSTOWN SHEET & TUBE	.8114	.8354	.8592	.7783	.8147	.8408
ZENITH RADIO	.3550	.7379	.7589	.2096	.7162	.7547

V

Diversification Within and Among
2-Digit Industry Groups

THE REGRESSION results reported in Chapter IV suggest
that it is entry or diversification *within* established
2-digit industry groups that may be growth-related, not
a broader or more conglomerate form of inter-industry
activity on the part of these 460 *Fortune* corporations.
But the entry and diversification variables employed in
that analysis fail to identify fully those inter-industry
shifts that are within as opposed to across 2-digit industry groups.

For example, entry into a new 2-digit industry group
necessarily involves entry to a new 4-digit industry. But it
could result in entry to several new 4-digit industries.
Similarly, increased diversification at the 2-digit level
would be expected, other things being equal, to lead to
increased diversification at the 4-digit level. But other
things may not be equal, and increasing 2-digit diversification *could* be accompanied by *decreasing* 4-digit
diversification. It is not likely, but it is possible.

ALTERNATIVE MEASURES OF CORPORATE
DIVERSIFICATION AND ENTRY

Accordingly, measures of 4-digit entry and of changing
4-digit diversification are here redefined as follows:

(1) *4-Digit Entry—Old 2-Digit Groups*: The number
of 4-digit industries in which the firm was active in 1965

91

but not in 1960, but which were 4-digit industries classified within 2-digit industry groups within which the firm
did have products in 1960. This variable measures entry
to 4-digit industries within "old" 2-digit categories—2-
digit industry groups in which the firm was already active
in 1960.

(2) *4-Digit Entry—New 2-Digit Groups*: The number of 4-digit industries in which the firm reported products in 1965 that were in 2-digit industry groups in
which the firm was *not* active in 1960. This variable
measures entry to 4-digit industries within "new" 2-digit
categories.

(3) *4-Digit Diversification to Old 2-Digit Groups—
Herfindahl*: The percentage change in the previously defined index of 4-digit diversification between 1960 and
1965, when the 1965 index is based only on estimated
employment *within* 2-digit industry groups in which the
firm reported products in 1960. This variable indicates
by how much the diversification of these firms would
have changed had all activity within entered 2-digit industry groups not occurred.[1]

(4) *4-Digit Diversification to New 2-Digit Groups—
Herfindahl*: The total percentage change in the previously
defined index of 4-digit diversification between 1960 and
1965 *minus* variable (3) above. This variable indicates
the contribution of estimated production in entered 2-
digit industry groups to the percentage change in the 4-
digit diversification of these firms.

[1] The Herfindahl Index is in each year defined as
$H = -\sum_{i=1}^{n} p_i^2$ where p_i is the share of the firm's estimated employment in the nth industry. Note that in the regressions *percentage* change in this measure is in each case the operational variable. Note also that in the Appendix to this chapter this index is
defined as $1 - \sum_{i=1}^{n} p_i^2$ so that values shown will range from 0 to 1.

92

(5) *4-Digit Diversification to Old 2-Digit Groups—Ash*: This variable is the absolute change between 1960 and 1965 in an index of diversification defined as $D = \sum_{i=1}^{n} p_i(\log 1/p_i)$ where p_i is the estimated proportion of the firm's productive activity in the ith 4-digit industry and where all productive activity by the firm within 2-digit industry groups in which the firm was not active in 1960 is ignored. This variable measures the extent to which this index of 4-digit diversification would have changed had the firm failed to enter any new 2-digit industry group. This particular index of diversification is suggested by Ash.[2]

(6) *4-Digit Diversification to New 2-Digit Groups—Ash*: This variable is the difference between the 1965 Ash index of 4-digit diversification (when the firm's total productive activity is considered) and the value of that index when activity within entered 2-digit industry groups is ignored. The variable indicates the degree to which 1965 diversification of the firm was increased by entry to 4-digit industries within "new" 2-digit industry groups.

Table 5-1 shows the mean values of these added variables. What is surprising in the light of the earlier measures is that 4-digit diversification involving new 2-digit industry groups led to substantially greater change overall

[2] See Robert Ash, *Information Theory* (New York: Interscience Publishers, 1965), pp. 5-8. As employed, the index is based on natural logarithms. Where production is equal among the n industries, this index will be equal to $\log_e 1/p_i$ or approximately 2.3 if n is 10. Note that the Ash index is not bounded as is the Herfindahl Index, and is therefore more sensitive to change in diversification in the case of initially highly diversified firms. Expressing change in the Herfindahl Index in percentage terms is an attempt to compensate for this deficiency. Change in the Ash index is introduced in absolute values.

than corresponding activity within the old or initial 2-digit categories. Indeed, with the Herfindahl-type index of diversification, the average percentage change in diversification at the 4-digit level is negative if only those 2-digit industry groups in which these firms (individually) had been active five years earlier are considered.[3] It was activ-

TABLE 5-1:

ENTRY AND CHANGING DIVERSIFICATION, MEANS VALUES
(UNWEIGHTED), 460 LARGE INDUSTRIAL CORPORATIONS,
1960-1965

Variable	*Mean Value*
4-Digit Entry:	
Total	3.98
To Old 2-Digit Groups	2.56
To New 2-Digit Groups	1.42
Percent Change in 4-Digit	
Diversification:[a] (Herfindahl)	
Total	4.99
To Old 2-Digit Groups	-1.38
To New 2-Digit Groups	6.37
Change in 4-Digit Diversification	
(Ash)	
Total	.149
To Old 2-Digit Groups	.049
To New 2-Digit Groups	.100

[a] The numbers shown are unweighted averages for the 460 corporations. Corresponding figures for individual corporations are contained in the Appendix to this chapter. See also text, note 3.

Source: Derived from data in *Fortune*, Market Research Department, *1961 Plant and Product Directory* (Time, Inc., 1961) and *1966 Plant and Product Directory* (Time, Inc., 1966).

[3] It is not true, however, that the average value of this Herfindahl Index fell if new 2-digit industries are ignored. The average value of this index for these firms was .627 in 1960 and .661 in

94

ity within new or entered 2-digit industry groups that led to most of the increased diversification by these corporations as a whole. That is particularly surprising since the average number of 4-digit industries entered that were in "new" 2-digit industry groups is substantially less than the number entered in old 2-digit categories.

REGRESSION RESULTS

Table 5-2 reports regression results from an analysis corresponding to that of Chapter IV, but employing these added variables. The findings are negative. Splitting 4-digit entry and diversification between new and old 2-digit industry groups fails to support the hypothesis that it is 4-digit inter-industry activity within old 2-digit categories that is primarily growth-related. In Table 5-2 coefficients are positive and significant on both components of 4-digit inter-industry activity. With the exception of regression (2), based on change in the Herfindahl-type index of 4-digit diversification, the coefficients themselves are very similar, and in the case of regression (2) the coefficient on diversification to new 2-digit categories exceeds, though not statistically significantly, that on diversification to 2-digit industry groups within which the firm was previously active. The clear implication is that both forms of diversification have been related to the growth rate of these firms.

Interestingly, however, the measures of inter-industry activity across and within 2-digit industry groups are not

---

1965. Basing the index only on "old" 2-digit industries in 1965 yields a value of .637. Corresponding averages for the Ash index are 1.455, 1.603, and 1.504. Note that Table 5-1 shows mean values for change in diversification, not change in mean diversification.

highly correlated one with another. The simple correlation coefficient (r) between the Ash indices of changing 4-digit diversification is only .057. The correlation coefficient between entry to 4-digit industries within old

TABLE 5-2:

REGRESSION COEFFICIENTS AND t-RATIOS, PERCENT CHANGE IN TOTAL ASSETS ON SELECTED INDEPENDENT VARIABLES, 460 LARGE INDUSTRIAL CORPORATIONS, 1960-1965

Independent Variable	Regression Coefficients and t-Ratios[a]		
	(1)	(2)	(3)
Log$_e$ Total Assets 1960	-10.34 (-5.07)	-7.08 (-3.36)	-7.90 (-3.89)
Earnings, 1960	1.65 (3.56)	1.31 (2.66)	1.19 (2.51)
Projected Growth	.211 (1.84)	.367 (3.06)	.356 (3.08)
4-Digit Entry to New 2-Digit Groups	3.32 (3.29)		
4-Digit Entry to Old 2-Digit Groups	3.63 (5.25)		
4-Digit Diversification (Herf.) New 2-Digit Groups		.425 (3.18)	
4-Digit Diversification (Herf.) Old 2-Digit Groups		.261 (3.96)	
4-Digit Diversification (Ash) New 2-Digit Groups			43.50 (3.89)
4-Digit Diversification (Ash) Old 2-Digit Groups			41.40 (6.51)
R^2	.19	.10	.17

[a] The t-ratios are shown in parentheses.

2-digit categories and 4-digit entry within new 2-digit industry groups is higher, but even then only 0.54. A matrix of these simple correlation coefficients is contained in Table 5-3. It seems not unlikely, therefore, that differ-

TABLE 5-3:

MATRIX OF SIMPLE CORRELATION COEFFICIENTS (r), SELECTED MEASURES OF 4-DIGIT INTER-INDUSTRY ACTIVITY, 460 CORPORATIONS, 1960-1965[a]

Variable	HOLD	HNEW	AOLD	ANEW	ENTOLD	ENTNW
HOLD	1.00	.14	.89	-.01	.27	.16
HNEW		1.00	-.09	.85	.02	.39
AOLD			1.00	.06	.44	.27
ANEW				1.00	.09	.64
ENTOLD					1.00	.54
ENTNW						1.00

[a]HOLD and HNEW are percent change in the Herfindahl index of diversification—to old and to new 2-digit industry groups respectively. AOLD and ANEW are change in the Ash index of diversification—also to old and to new 2-digit industry groups respectively. ENTOLD and ENTNW are 4-digit entry within old and new 2-digit industry groups respectively. These definitions are also given below in the text. See p. 98.

ent firms have found it advantageous to diversify into, or to enter, 4-digit industries either within or outside 2-digit industry groups in which they have already been active, depending upon the circumstances of the firm in question. The most plausible argument would be that the firms that face unfavorable growth opportunities within their established markets would be those most prone to diversify into unrelated markets, whereas firms with substantial potential for growth within their present markets would tend, in contrast, to expand (if they do so at all) to areas closely related to those markets.[4]

[4] This is a common and not particularly recent argument. See, for example, Edith T. Penrose, *The Theory of the Growth of*

The data fail to support that argument. Table 5-4 contains regression coefficients and *t*-ratios obtained by repeating the regressions of Table 5-2 for sub-sets of these

TABLE 5-4:

REGRESSION COEFFICIENTS AND *t*-RATIOS, PERCENT INCREASE IN
TOTAL ASSETS ON SELECTED INDEPENDENT VARIABLES, 460
CORPORATIONS RANKED BY PROJECTED GROWTH, 1960-1965

Sample	Independent Variable, Regression Coefficient,[a] and t-Ratios					
	Assets-Log	EARN 60	PROGRO	HOLD	HNEW	R^2
Top 230 Firms (1)	-10.69 (-3.34)	.63 (.91)	.458 (1.98)	.28 (2.94)	.22 (.87)	.10
Bottom 230 Firms (2)	-2.66 (-.98)	2.21 (3.19)	-.416 (-1.52)	.29 (3.15)	.51 (3.43)	.13
	Assets-Log	EARN 60	PROGRO	AOLD	ANEW	R^2
Top 230 Firms (3)	-10.34 (-3.34)	.48 (.72)	.387 (1.73)	51.12 (4.93)	37.41 (1.47)	.18
Bottom 230 Firms (4)	-4.28 (-1.60)	2.13 (3.16)	-.319 (-1.20)	33.65 (4.35)	40.18 (3.43)	.17
	Assets-Log	EARN 60	PROGRO	ENTOLD	ENTNW	R^2
Top 230 Firms (5)	-14.41 (-4.72)	1.25 (1.94)	.366 (1.72)	3.73 (3.94)	3.41 (2.28)	.23
Bottom 230 Firms (6)	-4.85 (-1.76)	2.33 (3.42)	-.313 (-1.16)	3.70 (3.41)	2.34 (1.70)	.15

[a]The *t*-ratios are shown in parentheses.

Firms (Oxford: Blackwell, 1959). See also Robin Marris, "A Model of the 'Managerial' Enterprise," *Quarterly Journal of Economics*, Vol. 77, May 1963, pp. 185-209.

firms when the firms are ranked in order of ascending values of the projected growth variable (PROGRO). On the one hand, the first two regressions shown, employing HOLD and HNEW—percent change in the 4-digit Herfindahl Index within old and new 2-digit industry groups respectively—do appear consistent with this interpretation. For firms with a high projected growth rate, the coefficient on 4-digit diversification within new 2-digit industries is not significant, whereas for those 230 corporations with the lowest projected industry growth rate, that coefficient is both large and significant. This is also true if the corresponding Ash measures of changing diversification—AOLD and ANEW—are substituted. In that event, however, the difference in the coefficients is more striking in the case of those firms with the highest rate of projected growth.

On the other hand, if measures of 4-digit entry are introduced—ENTOLD and ENTNW—such a pattern is not evident. Indeed, for those firms with the lowest PROGRO values, the coefficient on entry to 4-digit industries within new 2-digit industry groups is not statistically significant, whereas that on entry to 4-digit industries within old 2-digit categories is both high and significant.

Furthermore, even for the diversification measures, the pattern is not consistent if the division of these firms by their level of projected growth is extended to quartiles. Table 5-5 contains corresponding regression results with such a division of the sample of 460 firms. Table 5-6 is identical, except that the projected growth variable is omitted from each of the regressions. In each case, there is a tendency for the coefficients on within old 2-digit inter-industry variables to be more significant and larger the higher the level of the projected growth rate of the

115 firms except for the bottom 115 corporations. Within that bottom group, and regardless of the inter-industry variable employed, the pattern is reversed: coefficients on diversification or entry to new 2-digit categories are in general low and not significant while those on the corresponding measures within old 2-digit categories tend to be both high and significant.

TABLE 5-5:

REGRESSION COEFFICIENTS AND t-RATIOS, PERCENT CHANGE IN TOTAL ASSETS ON SELECTED INDEPENDENT VARIABLES, 460 CORPORATIONS RANKED BY PROJECTED GROWTH, 1960-1965

Sample	Independent Variable, Regression Coefficient, and t-Ratio[a]					
	Assets-Log	EARN 60	PROGRO	HOLD	HNEW	R^2
(1) Top 115	-9.53	.117	.468	.376	.360	.09
Corporations	(-1.88)	(.13)	(1.30)	(2.43)	(.73)	
(2) Second 115	-9.95	1.677	-3.227	.181	.214	.16
Corporations	(-2.50)	(1.53)	(-2.41)	(1.44)	(.73)	
(3) Third 115	-5.67	2.380	-3.290	.161	.507	.15
Corporations	(-1.40)	(2.63)	(-2.00)	(1.05)	(2.80)	
(4) Bottom 115	-.30	2.145	-.948	.397	.363	.17
Corporations	(-.08)	(2.00)	(-2.23)	(3.32)	(1.22)	
	Assets-Log	EARN 60	PROGRO	AOLD	ANEW	R^2
(1) Top 115	-9.37	.135	.361	57.43	54.72	.19
Corporations	(-1.94)	(.15)	(1.05)	(3.84)	(1.48)	
(2) Second 115	-9.69	1.310	-3.135	40.09	11.33	.20
Corporations	(-2.47)	(1.21)	(2.40)	(2.80)	(.33)	
(3) Third 115	-6.09	2.309	-3.171	21.55	53.65	.18
Corporations	(-1.52)	(2.60)	(-1.97)	(1.53)	(3.46)	
(4) Botton 115	-2.38	2.203	-.875	42.99	16.06	.24
Corporations	(-.64)	(2.16)	(-2.16)	(4.63)	(.89)	
	Assets-Log	EARN 60	PROGRO	ENTOLD	ENTNW	R^2
(1) Top 115	-14.77	.790	.481	5.072	4.94	.35
Corporations	(-3.39)	(1.00)	(1.58)	(4.26)	(2.75)	
(2) Second 115	-11.80	2.255	-3.743	2.599	.71	.18
Corporations	(-2.93)	(2.10)	(-2.80)	(1.67)	(.27)	
(3) Third 115	-9.02	2.221	-3.215	1.326	6.03	.18
Corporations	(-2.19)	(2.48)	(-1.97)	(.86)	(3.14)	
(4) Bottom 115	-1.46	3.155	-.665	7.825	-3.026	.27
Corporations	(-.41)	(3.19)	(-1.69)	(5.12)	(-1.56)	

[a]The t-ratios are shown in parentheses.

Diversification: 2-Digit Groups

For corporations other than those found in the most slow-growing industries, therefore, there is some support in these results for the Penrose-type hypothesis—that diversification is a response to unfavorable growth pros-

TABLE 5-6:

REGRESSION COEFFICIENTS AND t-RATIOS, PERCENT INCREASE IN TOTAL ASSETS ON SELECTED INDEPENDENT VARIABLES, 460 CORPORATIONS RANKED BY PROJECTED GROWTH, 1960-1965

Sample	Independent Variable, Regression Coefficient, and t-Ratio[a]				
	Assets-Log	EARN 60	HOLD	HNEW	R^2
(1) Top 115	-9.45	.125	.380	.438	.08
Corporations	(-1.86)	(.13)	(2.44)	(.90)	
(2) Second 115	-11.06	1.716	.171	.239	.12
Corporations	(-2.73)	(1.53)	(1.33)	(.73)	
(3) Third 115	-4.22	2.241	.142	.486	.12
Corporations	(-1.04)	(2.45)	(.91)	(2.65)	
(4) Bottom 115	-2.53	2.192	.383	.353	.13
Corporations	(-.69)	(2.00)	(2.98)	(1.17)	
	Assets-Log	EARN 60	AOLD	ANEW	R^2
(1) Top 115	-9.22	.133	56.94	62.45	.18
Corporations	(-1.91)	(.15)	(3.80)	(1.73)	
(2) Second 115	-10.76	1.331	40.60	12.02	.16
Corporations	(-2.70)	(1.20)	(2.78)	(.34)	
(3) Third 115	-4.67	2.178	20.02	53.39	.15
Corporations	(-1.17)	(2.43)	(1.41)	(3.40)	
(4) Bottom 115	-4.60	2.204	41.33	18.46	.20
Corporations	(-1.27)	(2.13)	(4.39)	(1.00)	
	Assets-Log	EARN 60	ENTOLD	ENTNW	R^2
(1) Top 115	-14.72	.795	4.92	5.19	.33
Corporations	(-3.36)	(1.00)	(4.12)	(2.88)	
(2) Second 115	-12.73	2.248	2.28	.32	.12
Corporations	(-3.07)	(2.03)	(1.43)	(.12)	
(3) Third 115	-7.40	2.132	.80	6.24	.15
Corporations	(-1.81)	(2.36)	(.52)	(3.22)	
(4) Bottom 115	-3.21	3.154	7.89	-2.99	.25
Corporations	(-.92)	(3.17)	(5.13)	(-1.54)	

[a] The t-ratios are shown in parentheses.

pects in the firm's current industries—but that pattern of behavior does not appear to extend to firms whose prospects are the worst in this regard. The evidence as a whole is not strong.

CORPORATE SIZE AND EARNINGS

More consistent in these tables is the behavior of the coefficients on the corporate size and earnings variables. The former tend to be large, negative, and significant only for those corporations in the more rapidly growing industries, whereas corporate earnings appear significant only in slowly growing industries. The hypothesis, if not supported, is at least suggested that, in terms of relative growth, corporate size has been the greatest disadvantage within rapidly growing industries, but that firms within such industries have had little difficulty expanding, regardless of their record of earnings. Corporate earnings, however, appear to have been an increasingly important determinant of corporate growth the less rapid the growth rates of the industries of the firms in question.

DIVERSIFICATION AS A DEPENDENT VARIABLE

The obvious alternative formulation is contained by Table 5-7. That table shows regression results for the 460 corporations when each of the foregoing measures of changing diversification and entry is used as a dependent variable, with corporate size, earnings, projected growth and actual growth (ACTGR) as independent variables. The earlier discussion suggests that diversification (or entry) to new 2-digit industry groups is likely to be higher the larger the firm, the less promising the growth of the firm's industry (or industries), the poorer the earnings record of the firm, and, presumably, the lower the actual growth of the firm. In the case of diversification (or entry) within old 2-digit industry groups, coefficients on the projected growth and earnings variables would be expected to be reversed. Interpretation of the results of these regressions has to be awkward. Coefficients of determination are exceed-

TABLE 5-7:

REGRESSION COEFFICIENTS AND t-RATIOS, 4-DIGIT INTER-INDUSTRY MEASURES ON SELECTED INDEPENDENT VARIABLES, 460 CORPORATIONS, 1960-1965[a]

Dependent Variable	Independent Variable [a]				
	Assets-Log	PROGRO	EARN 60	ACTGR	R^2
(1) HOLD	1.577	-.041	.875		.02
	(1.04)	(-.47)	(2.48)		
(2) HNEW	.105	.046	.049		.00
	(.14)	(1.08)	(.28)		
(3) HOLD	2.333	-.084	.697	.114	.04
	(1.55)	(-.97)	(1.98)	(3.51)	
(4) HNEW	.382	.030	-.017	.042	.02
	(.51)	(.71)	(.10)	(2.60)	
(5) AOLD	.025	.000	.008		.02
	(1.71)	(.05)	(2.22)		
(6) ANEW	.005	.000	.001		.00
	(.59)	(.88)	(.59)		
(7) AOLD	.039	.001	.005	.002	.10
	(2.71)	(.88)	(1.34)	(6.62)	
(8) ANEW	.010	.000	.004	.001	.04
	(1.17)	(.31)	(.00)	(4.05)	
(9) ENTOLD	.716	.033	-.012		.08
	(4.54)	(3.69)	(-.33)		
(10) ENTNW	.335	.013	-.013		.03
	(3.10)	(2.18)	(-.54)		
(11) ENTOLD	.887	.023	-.052	.026	.19
	(5.95)	(2.75)	(-1.51)	(8.04)	
(12) ENTNW	.436	.008	-.038	.015	.12
	(4.19)	(1.23)	(-1.55)	(6.82)	

[a] The t-ratios are shown in parentheses.

ingly low, and the coefficients on the variables included are interesting chiefly for their lack of significance. Nevertheless, for the diversification measures, t-ratios are marginally significant for coefficients on corporate earnings when the diversification is to 4-digit industries within the present (old) 2-digit industry groups of these firms. This is not the case, as expected, with 4-digit diversification to new 2-digit industry groups. Offsetting that, however, are ambiguous results in terms of the projected growth variable. Where differences are present, higher coefficients are obtained on this variable with diversification to new 2-digit industries. This is not the result that would be anticipated if low industry growth rates lead to diversification outside those industries. In no instance, however, are these coefficients significant by the usual tests.

If entry, rather than changing diversification, is the measure of 4-digit inter-industry activity, the picture is just the reverse. Coefficients on projected growth are significant and higher with entry to old 2-digit industry groups; no difference is apparent between entry to new and entry to old 2-digit categories in terms of the coefficients on corporate earnings. The evidence is mixed. It does suggest that both earnings and the projected growth rate variable are favorable indicators of a firm's market position, and that the two interact in the decision to diversify. The only highly significant coefficients in Table 5-7 are those on the actual growth rates of these corporations between 1960 and 1965, and those coefficients consistently show a greater relationship with diversification or entry *within* 2-digit categories. This is true also of the more marginally significant coefficients on corporate size. Other things being equal, there is, apparently, a greater tendency for corporate size and growth to generate 4-

digit diversification within established market areas. But the evidence is far from strong.

SUMMARY AND COMMENT

This chapter pursues, therefore, the work of Chapter IV in relating corporate growth to 4-digit entry and diversification. Its contribution is the development of measures that distinguish clearly between 4-digit entry and diversification within, and 4-digit entry and diversification among, 2-digit industry groups. Analysis relating corporate growth to those measures, however, fails to yield striking results. Increasing 4-digit diversification *is* related to corporate growth, but that is true regardless of whether the diversification is within or among 2-digit categories. Very slightly higher levels of significance are obtained with coefficients on the former measures, but the coefficients themselves are by no means significantly different. Corporate growth, during this period and for these 460 large industrial corporations, is shown to be associated positively with corporate earning, industry growth rates, and increasing 4-digit diversification (and entry), and to be negatively associated with corporate size.

If these corporations are ranked by the growth rates projected from the growth rates of the industries in which they were active in 1960, there is consistent evidence that the negative impact of corporate size on corporate growth declines (though it remains negative) as the level of projected growth declines. Conversely, the relationship with corporate earnings is apparent only where levels of projected growth are relatively low. There is only slight evidence in these data that diversification or entry to new 2-digit categories has been a response to low levels of projected growth, or to low levels of earnings, on the part of these firms.

105

Two Qualifications

There are two major caveats. The first is related to the nature of the analysis itself; the second is a consequence of the data employed. In terms of the analytic framework, much of the demonstrated slender association between diversification and corporate growth is to be expected. Large corporations are more apt to be diversified than small corporations. As a corporation grows, it is apt to diversify. A positive association with diversification is therefore scarcely earth-shaking. Similarly, where corporate earnings are retained in large part by large industrial corporations, where such retained earnings are at the very least carried as an addition to surplus, and where the measure of corporate growth is growth in the assets of these corporations, an association with corporate earnings is also scarcely surprising.

Much the same argument can be made with respect to corporate size. A given percentage increase in the assets of a corporation will be achieved with a smaller absolute increase in the assets of a small than a large firm. It would be surprising if the assets of the Exxon Corporation were to double in five years, yet the *average* growth of all these corporations between 1960 and 1965 was almost 50 percent. That, however, is beside the point. Substantial public interest attaches to the question of whether *this relative measure*—not some alternative measure—*has* been positively associated with corporate size. For the period considered here, and for these 460 corporations, the answer is no, although the quantitative impact of corporate size is not very great, about a 10 percentage point reduction for a doubling of corporate assets.[5]

[5] It should be clear that this conclusion extends only to rela-

The focus of the analysis, however, is not corporate size but corporate diversification. In this context, the underlying data cause difficulty. Change in 4-digit diversification, and measures of 4-digit entry, are calculated both within and across 2-digit industry groups. The rationale is that the former—the within 2-digit measures—indicate corporate activity within related markets, that such diversification or entry adds products to a firm's production that are not in general independent of those which characterize the firm's original or prior product mix. That diversification or entry is contrasted with the addition of products in 4-digit industries classified in 2-digit industry groups in which the firm was not previously active. Here the assumption is that products will tend to be totally new—not related on either the supply or the demand side to those previously characteristic of the firm in question.

In detail, these assumptions are wrong.[6] Four-digit industries within 2-digit industry groups can be very distinct. The manufacture of mattresses is quite different from the manufacture of wood television cabinets, yet both are classified within 2-digit industry group 25. Conversely, the manufacture of wood television cabinets is quite close to the manufacture of plastic television cabinets, yet these would be in different 2-digit industry groups.[7] Almost any number of similar illustrations could

---

tive growth *within* this group of 460 large corporations, not to any comparison involving smaller firms.

[6] They are also frequently accepted. See *Economic Report on Corporate Mergers*, Staff Report to the Federal Trade Commission (Government Printing Office, 1969), pp. 242-244.

[7] U.S. Bureau of the Budget, *Standard Industrial Classification Manual* (Government Printing Office, 1957).

be cited. The Standard Industrial Classification does not provide an error-free vehicle for this kind of segregation of the 4-digit industries of manufacturing. Much of the 4-digit diversification across 2-digit groups recorded earlier in this chapter *may* reflect vertical consolidation of industries within corporations, and *might* therefore link "closer" industries than would be true in the case of some within 2-digit 4-digit diversification.[8]

The preceding results fail to identify clearly a differential response of the growth rates of these corporations to 4-digit diversification within, as opposed to among, 2-digit industry groups. They do not guarantee that diversification by rapidly growing firms has not been primarily to markets which are interrelated one with another. They indicate only that, by the measures employed here, such a pattern of behavior is not readily isolated with publicly available data and with manipulation of those data within the framework of the Standard Industrial Classification.

[8] Several people, Lee E. Preston in particular, have suggested that an interesting variation of this work would involve a vertical reclassification of the SIC based on input-output tables, and the construction of indices of diversification and of changing diversification on that basis rather than on the basis of the 2-digit classification as here reported.

Appendix

Shown below are values, for each of the 460 corporations considered, of 1960 4-digit diversification and of changing 4-digit diversification between 1960 and 1965. Both Herfindahl and Ash indices are listed. The 1960 Herfindahl index is shown as $1 - \sum_{i=1}^{n} p_i^2$, where p_i is the estimated proportion of the firm's total employment which is within the ith 4-digit industry. *Change* in both the Herfindahl and Ash indices as in absolute terms. Adding the sum of the two measures given for changing diversification to the 1960 index yields, in each case, the 1965 index. Some interesting properties of these two indices are discussed, in a different context, in A. Jacquemin and A. M. Kumps, "Changes in the Size Structure of the Largest European Firms: An Entropy Measure," *The Journal of Industrial Economics*, November, 1971, pp. 59-68, esp. pp. 60 and 61.

Diversification: 2-Digit Groups

TABLE 5A-1

COMPANY NAME	HERFINDAHL INDEX			ASH INDEX		
	1960 INDEX	CHANGE, 1960-65 OLD 2-DIGIT	NEW 2-DIGIT	1960 INDEX	CHANGE, 1960-65 OLD 2-DIGIT	NEW 2-DIGIT
ACF INDUSTRIES	.9005	-.1354	0.0560	2.6400	-0.7084	0.2379
ABBOTT LABORATORIES	.7091	0.0721	-.0038	1.3234	0.2676	0.0727
ADDRESSOGRAPH-MULTIGRAPH	.8312	0.0148	0.0423	1.8934	0.1396	0.3193
ADMIRAL	.7118	0.0880	0.0	1.5421	0.3686	0.0
AIR REDUCTION	.1790	0.4740	0.0683	0.4918	1.1663	0.2285
ALAN WOOD STEEL	.4124	-.0548	0.0	0.8654	-0.1339	0.0
ALLEGHENY LUDLUM STEEL	.5323	0.0099	0.0	1.0538	0.0430	0.0
ALLIED CHEMICAL	.8318	0.0282	0.0238	2.1967	0.1235	0.1762
ALLIED MILLS	.1444	0.2757	0.0	0.2746	0.4649	0.0
ALLIS-CHALMERS	.8996	-.0041	0.0059	2.4934	0.0846	0.0853
ALUMINUM CO. OF AMERICA	.8105	-.0176	0.0	2.0104	-0.0531	0.0
AMERICAN BAKERIES	.1633	-.0928	0.0	0.3306	-0.1542	0.0
AMERICAN BOSCH ARMA	.7973	-.0490	0.0	1.8599	-0.2797	0.0
AMERICAN BRAKE SHOE	.8063	-.0091	0.0103	1.9327	-0.0314	0.0740
AMERICAN CAN	.7767	-.0147	0.0015	1.8153	0.0623	0.0150
AMERICAN CHAIN & CABLE	.8569	-.0173	0.0	2.3762	-0.1566	0.0
AMERICAN CYANAMID	.9174	-.0026	0.0064	2.6794	0.0897	0.1214
AMERICAN ENKA	.6843	0.0388	0.0	1.4347	0.0768	0.0
AMERICAN FOREST PRODUCTS	.7942	-.0325	0.0300	1.8394	-0.1870	0.2036
AMERICAN HOME PRODUCTS	.8208	-.0329	0.0190	1.7749	0.3110	0.1574
AMERICAN MACHINE & FOUNDRY	.9455	-.0076	0.0028	3.0562	-0.0170	0.0540
AMERICAN-MARIETTA	.7188	0.1601	0.0073	2.0293	0.4450	0.1021
AMERICAN METAL CLIMAX	.8918	0.0079	0.0271	2.3338	0.1294	0.4507
AMERICAN MOTORS	.2534	-.0163	0.0	0.5418	0.0451	0.0
AMERICAN OPTICAL	.8555	0.0004	0.0	2.0248	0.0070	0.0
AMERICAN PETROFINA	.0	0.0	0.0	0.0	0.0	0.0
AM. RADIATOR & STD. SANITARY	.8881	0.0020	0.0006	2.4521	0.0257	0.0135
AMERICAN SMELTING & REFINING	.8357	0.0212	0.0	1.9160	0.1675	0.0
AMERICAN STEEL FOUNDRIES	.7837	-.0942	0.0357	1.7524	-0.2143	0.1426
AMERICAN SUGAR REFINING	.1007	0.2966	0.0	0.2257	0.4625	0.0
AMERICAN TOBACCO	.4300	0.0339	0.0	0.6993	0.0339	0.0
ANACONDA	.7395	0.1226	0.0024	2.0323	0.3646	0.0357
ANCHOR HOCKING GLASS	.6199	0.0231	0.0721	1.2341	0.0122	0.2972
ANDERSON-PRICHARD OIL	.5000	-.5000	0.0	0.6931	-0.6931	0.0
ANHEUSER-BUSCH	.8067	-.0060	0.0	1.8848	-0.0894	0.0
ARCHER-DANIELS-MIDLAND	.8500	0.0206	0.0068	2.0576	0.1236	0.0701
ARMCO STEEL	.7674	-.0727	0.0	1.6487	-0.0580	0.0
ARMOUR	.7924	-.0536	0.0920	2.0294	-0.0053	0.4499
ARMSTRONG CORK	.8460	0.0071	0.0144	2.1280	0.0520	0.0993
ARMSTRONG RUBBER	.0950	-.0950	0.0	0.1985	-0.1985	0.0

TABLE 5A-1 (CONT.)

COMPANY NAME	HERFINDAHL INDEX			ASH INDEX		
	1960 INDEX	CHANGE, 1960-65 OLD 2-DIGIT	NEW 2-DIGIT	1960 INDEX	CHANGE, 1960-65 OLD 2-DIGIT	NEW 2-DIGIT
ASHLAND OIL & REFINING	.3499	-.1072	0.3979	0.5344	-0.1271	0.7647
ATLANTIC REFINING	.7474	-.0005	0.0	1.3811	-0.0010	0.0
AVCO	.8860	0.0133	0.0206	2.4434	0.0632	0.2192
AVON PRODUCTS	.0	0.0	0.3047	0.0	0.0	0.4826
BABCOCK & WILCOX	.8372	0.0615	0.0	2.0578	0.4485	0.0
BEATRICE FOODS	.4934	0.2998	0.0090	1.2212	0.7334	0.0916
BEAUNIT MILLS	.7743	0.0562	0.0	1.9039	0.0926	0.0
BEECH AIRCRAFT	.7778	-.1126	0.0	1.5415	-0.4450	0.0
BEECH-NUT LIFE SAVERS	.6250	0.1225	0.0571	1.1201	0.3272	0.3017
BEMIS BROS. BAG	.8087	0.0863	0.0331	1.9283	0.8248	0.4194
BENDIX AVIATION	.9400	0.0040	0.0	3.2668	0.0382	0.0
BETHLEHEM STEEL	.8974	0.0037	0.0045	2.4612	0.1303	0.0681
BIBB MANUFACTURING	.7370	0.0021	0.0	1.5424	0.0397	0.0
BIGELOW-SANFORD CARPET	.7262	-.0614	0.0	1.3938	-0.2980	0.0
BLAW-KNOX	.8916	-.0246	0.0059	2.5099	-0.2382	0.0742
BLISS /E.W./	.7480	0.1050	0.0140	1.8485	0.3934	0.1219
BOEING AIRPLANE	.5465	0.0351	0.0	1.0421	-0.0292	0.0
BORDEN	.6075	0.1994	0.0231	1.4298	0.8196	0.1526
BORG-WARNER	.9233	-.0017	0.0011	3.0277	-0.0080	0.0259
BOTANY INDUSTRIES	.8112	-.2312	-.2276	1.9370	-0.8481	-0.3053
BRIGGS & STRATTON	.6667	0.0	0.0	1.0986	0.0	0.0
BRISTOL-MYERS	.6531	-.0768	0.0270	1.0790	-0.1484	0.1498
BROWN SHOE	.2796	-.0503	0.0375	0.5598	-0.0714	0.1047
BRUNSWICK-BALKE-COLLENDER	.6573	0.1166	0.0062	1.4285	0.3598	0.0494
BUCYRUS-ERIE	.1454	0.0459	0.0332	0.2762	0.0643	0.0947
BUDD	.7981	-.1149	0.0141	2.0141	-0.6126	0.0904
BURLINGTON INDUSTRIES	.8753	-.0114	0.0	2.3551	-0.1011	0.0
BURROUGHS	.6005	-.4474	0.0482	1.3699	-0.9359	0.1628
BUTLER MANUFACTURING	.4587	0.2021	0.0532	0.8742	0.4114	0.1938
CALIFORNIA PACKING	.2961	-.0260	0.0	0.7217	-0.0644	0.0
CALUMET & HECLA	.9171	-.0245	0.0078	2.5446	-0.0839	0.0855
CAMPBELL SOUP	.7049	0.0641	0.0	1.2981	0.2782	0.0
CAMPBELL TAGGART ASS. BKRIES	.0096	0.1306	0.0	0.0305	0.2380	0.0
CANADA DRY	.5088	0.0076	0.0	0.7379	0.0528	0.0
CANNON MILLS	.5312	-.1736	0.0	0.9003	-0.1688	0.0
CARBORUNDUM	.6221	0.0489	0.0034	1.5616	-0.0194	0.0246
CAREY /PHILIP/ MANUFACTURING	.7864	-.0009	0.0	1.6880	0.0711	0.0
CARNATION	.7814	0.0192	0.0	1.6832	0.1113	0.0
CARRIER	.6267	-.1457	0.0	1.2322	-0.1898	0.0
CASE /J.I./	.5519	0.0538	0.0	1.1095	-0.0708	0.0

TABLE 5A-1 (CONT.)

COMPANY NAME	HERFINDAHL INDEX			ASH INDEX		
	1960 INDEX	CHANGE, 1960-65 OLD 2-DIGIT	NEW 2-DIGIT	1960 INDEX	CHANGE, 1960-65 OLD 2-DIGIT	NEW 2-DIGIT
CATERPILLAR TRACTOR	.4225	0.1522	0.0	0.6135	0.3438	0.0
CECO STEEL PRODUCTS	.4145	0.0470	0.0950	0.7441	0.0462	0.2508
CELANESE	.6995	0.0319	0.0344	1.4846	0.0873	0.1929
CELOTEX	.7735	-.1186	0.2165	1.5348	-0.3530	1.0234
CENTRAL SOYA	.4944	-.0276	0.0	0.6875	-0.0279	0.0
CERRO DE PASCO	.7913	-.0140	0.0	1.7848	-0.1054	0.0
CERTAIN-TEED PRODUCTS	.5691	0.1265	0.0912	1.2387	0.0518	0.3663
CESSNA AIRCRAFT	.6675	0.0716	0.0	1.3060	0.2772	0.0
CHAMPION PAPER & FIBRE	.8606	0.0008	0.0009	2.0553	0.0699	0.0156
CHAMPION SPARK PLUG	.4800	0.0	0.0	0.6730	0.0	0.0
CHANCE VOUGHT AIRCRAFT	.7790	0.0707	0.0204	1.6138	0.4213	0.1853
CHEMETRON	.7445	-.3320	0.0039	1.8679	-0.7188	0.0186
CHICAGO PNEUMATIC TOOL	.8719	0.0181	0.0	2.1261	0.2216	0.0
CHRYSLER	.4701	0.0343	0.0005	1.0799	0.1054	0.0042
CINCINNATI MILLING MACHINE	.8733	0.0078	0.0	2.3299	0.0866	0.0
CITIES SERVICE	.3293	0.4518	0.0485	0.7188	1.2809	0.3662
CLARK EQUIPMENT	.7825	-.0039	0.0277	1.6196	0.0245	0.1476
CLARK OIL & REFINING	.0	0.0	0.6667	0.0	0.0	1.0986
CLEVELAND-CLIFFS IRON	.0	0.0	0.0	0.0	0.0	0.0
CLEVITE	.7395	0.1218	0.0157	1.7306	0.3961	0.1384
CLUETT, PEABODY	.7360	-.2002	0.0	1.8117	-0.6948	0.0
COCA-COLA	.3032	0.2156	0.0	0.6626	0.2858	0.0
COLGATE-PALMOLIVE	.5992	0.0075	0.0	0.9785	0.0149	0.0
COLLINS RADIO	.6409	-.0074	0.0811	1.0567	-0.0132	0.2702
COLORADO FUEL & IRON	.8288	-.0198	0.0072	2.0645	-0.1594	0.0605
COLORADO MILLING & ELEVATOR	.2166	0.0160	0.0	0.3740	0.0205	0.0
COMBUSTION ENGINEERING	.7200	-.0170	0.0	1.3229	0.0970	0.0
CONE MILLS	.3107	0.1077	0.0621	0.4896	0.2507	0.2428
CONSOLIDATED CIGAR	.0476	-.0159	0.1197	0.1147	-0.0321	0.2712
CONS. ELECTRONICS INDUSTRIES	.8446	0.0182	0.0109	2.2072	0.2427	0.1036
CONS. WATER POWER & PAPER	.6530	0.0345	0.0182	1.3108	0.1334	0.0939
CONSOLIDATION COAL	.6542	-.0678	-.3496	1.3783	-0.3973	-0.3939
CONSUMERS COOPERATIVE ASSOC.	.8622	-.1200	0.0078	2.2539	-0.3826	0.0514
CONTAINER CORP. OF AMERICA	.7819	-.0484	0.0280	1.9086	-0.3560	0.1355
CONTINENTAL BAKING	.2160	0.0136	0.0	0.4953	-0.0020	0.0
CONTINENTAL CAN	.8050	-.0322	0.0	2.1171	-0.0554	0.0
CONTINENTAL MOTORS	.6164	0.1239	0.0169	1.3639	0.3071	0.0944
CONTINENTAL OIL	.2080	0.6207	0.0299	0.4865	1.5301	0.2254
COPPERWELD STEEL	.6002	0.0198	0.0	1.2663	-0.1562	0.0
CORN PRODUCTS	.6897	0.0536	0.0	1.5629	0.1687	0.0

112

TABLE 5A-1 (CONT.)

COMPANY NAME	HERFINDAHL INDEX			ASH INDEX		
	1960 INDEX	CHANGE, 1960-65 OLD 2-DIGIT	NEW 2-DIGIT	1960 INDEX	CHANGE, 1960-65 OLD 2-DIGIT	NEW 2-DIGIT
CORNING GLASS WORKS	.5721	-.1966	0.0120	1.1406	-0.2254	0.0524
CRANE	.8206	-.0512	0.0151	2.0482	-0.1906	0.1103
CROWN CORK & SEAL	.5254	0.0781	0.0	1.0936	-0.0869	0.0
CROWN ZELLERBACH	.8456	-.0039	0.0056	1.9962	0.0175	0.0733
CRUCIBLE STEEL	.7783	0.0148	0.0448	1.6686	0.0753	0.2399
CUDAHY PACKING	.8025	-.0075	0.0	1.7975	-0.0864	0.0
CUMMINS ENGINE	.0899	0.2674	0.0946	0.2141	0.5083	0.2247
CURTIS PUBLISHING	.6176	-.0239	0.0	1.0778	-0.1035	0.0
CURTISS-WRIGHT	.8970	0.0044	0.0047	2.6144	-0.1188	0.0585
CUTLER-HAMMER	.8285	-.0868	0.0311	1.9671	-0.3901	0.1465
DAN RIVER MILLS	.7481	0.0390	0.0	1.5571	0.1710	0.0
DANA	.6924	0.1258	0.0147	1.3985	0.5284	0.0997
DAYCO	.8311	-.1448	0.1061	2.0108	-0.5896	0.4406
DEERE	.5328	-.0220	0.0	1.1050	-0.1023	0.0
DETROIT STEEL	.1068	-.1068	0.0	0.2175	-0.2175	0.0
DI GIORGIO FRUIT	.8260	-.0023	0.0	1.9631	-0.0188	0.0
DIAMOND ALKALI	.7876	0.0666	0.0102	1.7399	0.3410	0.0867
DIAMOND NATIONAL	.8865	0.0132	0.0055	2.3233	0.1207	0.0900
DOLE	.6942	0.0481	0.0123	1.2883	0.4383	0.0875
DONNELLEY /R.R./ & SONS	.5952	0.0	0.0	0.9965	0.0	0.0
DOUGLAS AIRCRAFT	.6064	0.1122	0.0	0.9936	0.3346	0.0
DOW CHEMICAL	.8924	0.0537	0.0066	2.4443	0.6072	0.1530
DRESSER INDUSTRIES	.8607	0.0364	0.0134	2.2876	0.2166	0.1616
DU PONT /E.I./ DE NEMOURS	.9128	-.0025	0.0	2.8932	-0.0876	0.0
EAGLE-PICHER	.9271	0.0191	0.0048	2.8174	0.2767	0.0844
EASTERN GAS & FUEL ASSOCIATES	.0	0.0	0.0	0.0	0.0	0.0
EASTERN STATES FARMERS EXCH.	.5983	0.1644	0.0	0.9933	0.5808	0.0
EASTMAN KODAK	.8495	-.0069	0.0	2.0295	-0.0762	0.0
EATON MANUFACTURING	.6563	0.1998	0.0067	1.7134	0.8013	0.0788
EKCO PRODUCTS	.8386	0.0470	0.0116	2.0146	0.3188	0.0924
ELECTRIC AUTOLITE	.8876	0.0012	0.0058	2.5369	-0.0472	0.0965
ELECTRIC STORAGE BATTERY	.5732	-.0136	0.0266	1.4781	-0.0478	0.0957
EMERSON ELEC. MANUFACTURING	.8824	-.0612	0.0181	2.2101	-0.0019	0.0968
ENDICOTT JOHNSON	.5184	-.2580	0.0	1.0817	-0.6524	0.0
ENGELHARD INDUSTRIES	.8721	0.0160	0.0	2.3510	-0.0359	0.0
EVANS PRODUCTS	.8379	0.0132	0.0	1.9162	0.3439	0.0
EX-CELL-O	.8531	0.0174	0.0122	2.2205	-0.0379	0.1058
FAIRBANKS WHITNEY	.9045	-.0064	0.0057	2.5442	-0.0020	0.0624
FAIRCHILD ENGINE & AIRPLANE	.7733	-.2330	0.0	1.7445	-0.6223	0.0
FAIRMONT FOODS	.6091	0.1087	0.0	1.1213	0.3286	0.0

TABLE 5A-1 (CONT.)

COMPANY NAME	HERFINDAHL INDEX			ASH INDEX		
	1960 INDEX	CHANGE, 1960-65		1960 INDEX	CHANGE, 1960-65	
		OLD 2-DIGIT	NEW 2-DIGIT		OLD 2-DIGIT	NEW 2-DIGIT
FALSTAFF BREWING	.0	0.1420	0.0	0.0	0.2712	0.0
FEDERAL-MOGUL-BOWER BEARINGS	.7101	0.0894	0.0552	1.4462	0.3477	0.3757
FEDERAL PAPER BOARD	.6825	0.0024	0.0	1.2066	0.0185	0.0
FIBREBOARD PAPER PRODUCTS	.8687	-.0203	0.0	2.2924	-0.1235	0.0
FIRESTONE TIRE & RUBBER	.9223	-.0651	0.0025	2.7842	-0.2450	0.0284
FLINTKOTE	.9258	-.0014	0.0	2.7729	-0.0431	0.0
FOOD MACHINERY & CHEMICAL	.9091	0.0090	0.0193	2.7576	0.1176	0.2875
FORD MOTOR	.6180	0.0007	0.0039	1.5836	0.1996	0.0233
FOREMOST DAIRIES	.6811	-.0063	0.0	1.3660	-0.1007	0.0
FOSTER WHEELER	.6087	-.3043	0.0	1.1830	-0.6332	0.0
FRUEHAUF TRAILER	.0861	0.5112	0.0144	0.2067	0.8494	0.0845
GARDNER-DENVER	.8476	0.0178	0.0	2.1435	0.1026	0.0
GENERAL AMER. TRANSPORTATION	.8549	-.0255	0.0055	2.1789	0.0039	0.0490
GENERAL ANILINE & FILM	.8469	-.0281	0.0415	2.0793	-0.0439	0.2342
GENERAL BAKING	.0	0.2083	0.0	0.0	0.3632	0.0
GENERAL CABLE	.3952	0.0016	0.0557	1.0131	-0.0235	0.1766
GENERAL DYNAMICS	.8253	0.0907	0.0006	2.3769	0.3872	0.0151
GENERAL ELECTRIC	.9530	0.0099	0.0011	3.5616	0.1687	0.0108
GENERAL FOODS	.8458	-.0072	0.0100	2.4135	-0.1105	0.0919
GENERAL MILLS	.8414	-.0119	0.0	2.2225	-0.1407	0.0
GENERAL MOTORS	.7870	-.0157	0.0026	2.5561	-0.0447	0.0244
GENERAL PRECISION EQUIPMENT	.9199	-.0052	0.0	2.7841	-0.0671	0.0
GEN. TELEPHONE & ELECTRONICS	.9166	0.0074	0.0020	2.7450	0.1063	0.0341
GENERAL TIRE & RUBBER	.8618	0.0231	0.0195	2.3233	0.1447	0.2296
GENESCO	.6817	0.1595	0.0144	1.7148	0.5826	0.1230
GEORGIA-PACIFIC	.5286	0.3700	0.0156	0.8414	1.6436	0.1726
GERBER PRODUCTS	.8061	-.0429	0.0164	1.6836	-0.1224	0.1030
GILLETTE	.5417	-.0988	0.0713	0.8877	-0.1347	0.2028
GLEN ALDEN	.5400	-.5400	0.7101	0.8979	-0.8979	1.3061
GLIDDEN	.7306	0.0878	0.0169	1.6004	0.4264	0.1370
GOODRICH /B.F./	.8242	0.0156	0.0	2.2943	0.0215	0.0
GOODYEAR TIRE & RUBBER	.8164	0.0133	0.0152	1.9338	0.2098	0.1412
GRACE /W.R./	.8867	0.0038	0.0221	2.6955	-0.1307	0.2518
GRANITE CITY STEEL	.5000	0.0	0.0	0.6931	0.0	0.0
GREAT WESTERN SUGAR	.0	0.0	0.0997	0.0	0.0	0.2062
GRINNELL	.6020	0.1394	0.0275	1.1944	0.3549	0.1653
GRUMMAN AIRCRAFT ENGINEERING	.6966	0.0330	0.0042	1.3009	0.0951	0.0352
GULF OIL	.0	0.0512	0.4352	0.0	0.1217	0.9998
HANDY & HARMAN	.6665	-.0038	0.0	1.0983	-0.0055	0.0
HANNA MINING	.4338	-.0730	0.0	0.7481	-0.1017	0.0

114

TABLE 5A-1 (CONT.)

COMPANY NAME	HERFINDAHL INDEX 1960 INDEX	CHANGE, 1960-65 OLD 2-DIGIT	CHANGE, 1960-65 NEW 2-DIGIT	ASH INDEX 1960 INDEX	CHANGE, 1960-65 OLD 2-DIGIT	CHANGE, 1960-65 NEW 2-DIGIT
HARBISON-WALKER REFRACTORIES	.5697	0.0439	0.0	0.9203	0.0922	0.0
HARNISCHFEGER	.7053	-.1046	0.0	1.3654	-0.3759	0.0
HARSCO	.8754	0.0117	0.0134	2.2461	0.2156	0.1305
HART SCHAFFNER & MARX	.7589	-.0089	0.0	1.5671	-0.1808	0.0
HEINZ /H.J./	.7771	0.0086	0.0	1.5441	0.0259	0.0
HERCULES POWDER	.8224	0.0078	0.0392	2.0774	0.0743	0.2269
HERSHEY CHOCOLATE	.0	0.1800	0.0	0.0	0.3251	0.0
HOOKER CHEMICAL	.7646	0.0337	0.0447	1.7070	0.1047	0.2607
HORMEL /GEORGE A./	.2812	0.2052	0.0	0.4547	0.2248	0.0
HOUDAILLE INDUSTRIES	.9036	0.0099	0.0	2.7501	-0.0511	0.0
HOWE SOUND	.8951	-.0190	0.0022	2.7211	-0.1938	0.0292
HUMBLE OIL & REFINING	.4528	0.0034	0.0	0.6452	0.1729	0.0
HUNT FOODS & INDUSTRIES	.8552	0.0081	0.0	2.2589	0.1436	0.0
HUPP	.8208	0.0653	0.0150	1.9343	0.4848	0.1615
HYGRADE FOOD PRODUCTS	.5752	0.0390	0.0	1.1775	-0.0438	0.0
I-T-E CIRCIUT BREAKER	.6639	-.0066	0.0750	1.5440	-0.1403	0.2148
IDEAL CEMENT	.1167	-.0818	0.0	0.2959	-0.2067	0.0
INGERSOLL-RAND	.8571	0.0071	0.0	2.0958	-0.0149	0.0
INLAND CONTAINER	.0	0.0	0.0	0.0	0.0	0.0
INLAND STEEL	.7517	0.0205	0.0	1.4917	0.2151	0.0
INTERCHEMICAL	.7556	0.0164	0.0	1.9100	-0.0623	0.0
INTERLAKE IRON	.0	0.2545	0.4612	0.0	0.5461	1.3938
INTERNAT. BUSINESS MACHINES	.5539	-.0431	0.0	1.0794	-0.0448	0.0
INTERNATIONAL HARVESTER	.8327	-.0490	0.0113	2.0331	-0.0409	0.1008
INTERNAT. MINERALS & CHEMICAL	.8390	-.2622	0.0	2.2174	-0.6812	0.0
INTERNATIONAL PAPER	.8361	-.0547	0.0068	2.2071	-0.2510	0.0516
INTERNATIONAL SHOE	.3242	-.0330	0.0125	0.7483	-0.0897	0.0506
INTERNATIONAL TEL. & TEL.	.5081	0.2475	0.0811	1.1739	0.8073	0.4788
INTERSTATE BAKERIES	.0	0.0	0.0	0.0	0.0	0.0
ISLAND CREEK COAL	.0	0.0	0.0	0.0	0.0	0.0
JOHNS-MANVILLE	.8561	0.0217	0.0198	2.1792	0.1422	0.1869
JOHNSON & JOHNSON	.7988	0.0184	0.0194	1.9736	0.0668	0.1350
JONES & LAUGHLIN STEEL	.7526	-.0712	0.0137	1.6816	-0.2272	0.0958
JOSLYN MJF. & SUPPL	.8661	0.0058	0.C	2.2613	-0.0366	0.C
JOY MANUFACTURING	.7746	0.0170	0.0070	1.7455	0.0475	0.0571
KAISER ALUMINUM & CHEMICAL	.8171	-.0344	0.0	1.9280	0.0106	0.0
KAISER INDUSTRIES	.4788	-.0906	0.0	1.1180	-0.1410	0.0
KAISER STEEL	.7425	-.0071	0.0	1.6356	0.0009	0.0
KAYSER-ROTH	.8605	0.0311	0.0	2.3933	0.2058	0.0
KELLOGG	.4511	0.0117	0.0	0.7111	-0.0556	0.0

TABLE 5A-1 (CONT.)

COMPANY NAME	HERFINDAHL INDEX			ASH INDEX		
	1960 INDEX	CHANGE, 1960-65		1960 INDEX	CHANGE, 1960-65	
		OLD 2-DIGIT	NEW 2-DIGIT		OLD 2-DIGIT	NEW 2-DIGIT
KELSEY-HAYES	.8296	-.0563	0.0	1.9685	-0.1849	0.0
KENDALL	.8413	0.0149	0.0029	1.9829	0.1472	0.0365
KENNECOTT COPPER	.7198	-.0104	0.0	1.4113	-0.1092	0.0
KERR-MCGEE OIL INDUSTRIES	.7129	-.0431	0.1133	1.3623	-0.0601	0.4364
KEYSTONE STEEL & WIRE	.5462	-.0303	0.0351	1.3260	-0.0208	0.1131
KIMBERLY-CLARK	.7399	-.0292	0.0548	1.8197	-0.2916	0.2568
KOPPERS	.7577	0.1278	0.0238	1.7345	0.6497	0.2314
KROEHLER MANUFACTURING	.4924	-.0221	0.0	0.8920	0.0597	0.0
LACLEDE STEEL	.6349	0.0030	0.0	1.0466	0.0078	0.0
LEAR	.8948	-.0056	0.0147	2.3277	0.0292	0.1499
LEHIGH PORTLAND CEMENT	.0	0.0476	0.0	0.0	0.1147	0.0
LEVER BROTHERS	.6123	-.0209	0.0	1.2145	-0.1402	0.0
LIBBEY-OWENS-FORD GLASS	.0253	-.0006	0.0	0.0686	-0.0014	0.0
LIBBY, MCNEILL & LIBBY	.6901	-.2333	0.0	1.3693	-0.4681	0.0
LIGGETT & MYERS TOBACCO	.4152	0.0292	0.0542	0.6058	0.0307	0.1727
LILLY /ELI/	.7073	0.0176	0.0	1.3498	0.0479	0.0
LILY TULIP CUP	.2331	-.0585	0.0703	0.4740	-0.0975	0.1662
LINK-BELT	.7946	0.0018	0.0	1.8404	0.0287	0.0
LIPTON /THOMAS J./	.3427	0.3293	0.0	0.6205	0.6782	0.0
LOCKHEED AIRCRAFT	.8085	-.0517	0.0064	1.9299	-0.0773	0.0467
LONE STAR CEMENT	.0	0.0	0.0	0.0	0.0	0.0
LONE STAR STEEL	.6400	-.1400	0.0	1.0549	-0.3618	0.0
LORILLARD /P./	.3750	0.1250	0.0	0.5623	0.3053	0.0
LOWENSTEIN /M./ & SONS	.5557	0.0209	0.0	1.1739	0.0235	0.0
LUKENS STEEL	.6667	0.0	0.0	1.0986	0.0	0.0
MACK TRUCKS	.0	0.0	0.0	0.0	0.0	0.0
MAGNAVOX	.6975	-.0326	0.1189	1.2489	-0.1528	0.5693
MALLORY /P.R./	.8250	-.2087	0.0	2.0724	-0.6530	0.0
MASONITE	.0220	-.0220	0.4179	0.0610	-0.0610	0.6695
MAYER /OSCAR/	.5369	-.0137	0.0	0.8350	-0.0256	0.0
MAYTAG	.0	0.0	0.0	0.0	0.0	0.0
MCCALL	.5348	0.2529	0.0	0.8486	0.7468	0.0
MCDONNELL AIRCRAFT	.8750	-.0417	0.0	2.0794	-0.2876	0.0
MCGRAW-EDISON	.9059	0.0015	0.0053	2.6923	-0.0038	0.0590
MCGRAW-HILL PUBLISHING	.6667	0.0	0.0	1.0986	0.0	0.0
MCLOUTH STEEL	.0	0.0	0.0	0.0	0.0	0.0
MEAD	.8464	0.0167	0.0128	2.0172	0.0847	0.1360
MERCK	.8009	-.0136	0.0	1.8600	-0.2464	0.0
MERITT-CHAPMAN & SCOTT	.8513	-.1205	0.0	2.1088	-0.6517	0.0
MIDLAND-ROSS	.8439	0.0448	0.0232	2.1094	0.3115	0.2613

TABLE 5A-1 (CONT.)

COMPANY NAME	HERFINDAHL INDEX			ASH INDEX		
	1960 INDEX	CHANGE, 1960-65 OLD 2-DIGIT	NEW 2-DIGIT	1960 INDEX	CHANGE, 1960-65 OLD 2-DIGIT	NEW 2-DIGIT
MILES LABORATORIES	.2192	0.1281	0.1388	0.4916	0.2492	0.4232
MINNEAPOLIS-HONEYWELL REG.	.8877	0.0033	0.0	2.3948	0.0017	0.0
MINNESOTA MINING & MFG.	.9482	-.0136	0.0	3.1600	-0.2260	0.0
MINNESOTA & ONTARIO PAPER	.5348	0.3439	0.0051	0.8486	1.4483	0.0798
MOHASCO INDUSTRIES	.7589	0.0596	-.0049	1.5814	0.2419	0.3005
MONSANTO CHEMICAL	.8517	0.0322	-.0176	2.1562	0.2215	0.0022
MORRELL /JOHN/	.5721	-.0539	0.0	1.0048	-0.1160	0.0
MOTOROLA	.6641	0.0524	0.0028	1.3010	0.2008	0.0243
NATIONAL BISCUIT	.4846	0.0586	0.0173	1.1551	0.1568	0.0834
NATIONAL CAN	.0	0.0	0.0333	0.0	0.0	0.0859
NATIONAL CASH REGISTER	.6797	0.0302	0.0414	1.2211	0.2236	0.1715
NATIONAL DAIRY PRODUCTS	.7626	-.0190	0.0	1.7099	0.0480	0.0
NATIONAL DISTILLERS & CHEM	.7019	0.0349	0.0971	1.6341	0.1286	0.5819
NATIONAL GYPSUM	.8117	-.0084	0.0140	2.0048	-0.1075	0.1156
NATIONAL HOMES	.0987	0.0943	0.0	0.2046	0.1899	0.0
NATIONAL LEAD	.8987	-.0083	0.0030	2.5738	-0.0244	0.0474
NATIONAL STEEL	.1276	-.0407	0.0	0.3330	-0.1010	0.0
NATIONAL SUGAR REFINING	.0	0.0	0.0	0.0	0.0	0.0
NEW YORK TIMES	.0	0.0	0.0	0.0	0.0	0.0
NEWPORT NEWS SHIPBUILDING	.5000	0.0	0.0	0.6931	0.0	0.0
NORTH AMERICAN AVIATION	.8129	0.0076	0.0406	1.8544	0.0168	0.3312
NORTHROP	.7884	0.0689	0.0152	1.7537	0.4832	0.1456
NORTHWESTERN STEEL & WIRE	.5000	0.0	0.0	0.6931	0.0	0.0
NORTON	.8148	0.0945	0.0117	1.9216	0.6566	0.1309
OHIO OIL	.4200	-.2817	0.3774	0.6109	-0.3452	0.5563
OLIN MATHIESON CHEMICAL	.9473	0.0031	0.0052	3.1606	0.0728	0.1169
OTIS ELEVATOR	.0	0.0	0.0	0.0	0.0	0.0
OUTBOARD MARINE	.2583	0.5365	0.0281	0.5647	1.1047	0.1555
OWENS-CORNING FIBERGLAS	.6498	-.0078	0.0146	1.1362	-0.0147	0.0791
OWENS-ILLINOIS GLASS	.7184	-.0445	0.0068	1.6860	-0.1650	0.0428
OXFORD PAPER	.3750	-.3750	0.0	0.5623	-0.5623	0.0
PABST BREWING	.3235	-.0455	0.0	0.6463	-0.0391	0.0
PACIFIC CAR & FOUNDRY	.8677	-.0062	0.0	2.2653	0.0264	0.0
PARKE, DAVIS	.7326	0.0484	0.0	1.3517	0.2040	0.0
PEABODY COAL	.0	0.0	0.0	0.0	0.0	0.0
PENNSALT CHEMICALS	.8914	-.0116	0.0261	2.3017	-0.0937	0.3233
PEPSI-COLA	.1424	-.1424	0.0	0.3122	-0.3122	0.0
PERMANENTE CEMENT	.6686	-.0395	0.1001	1.3690	-0.2472	0.4760
PET MILK	.6694	0.1444	0.0	1.2839	0.4935	0.0
PFIZER /CHAS./	.7254	0.0035	0.0648	1.3872	0.2294	0.3663

TABLE 5A-1 (CONT.)

COMPANY NAME	HERFINDAHL INDEX			ASH INDEX		
	1960 INDEX	CHANGE, 1960-65 OLD 2-DIGIT	NEW 2-DIGIT	1960 INDEX	CHANGE, 1960-65 OLD 2-DIGIT	NEW 2-DIGIT
PHELPS DODGE	.6492	-.0270	0.0658	1.1950	-0.0275	0.3518
PHILADELPHIA & READING	.8528	0.0230	-.0039	2.2071	0.0710	0.0506
PHILIP MORRIS	.7889	-.0837	0.0340	1.9226	-0.2132	0.1885
PHILLIPS PETROLEUM	.6280	0.0376	0.1449	1.5196	0.0563	0.4049
PILLSBURY	.6361	-.0005	0.0	1.2787	-0.0220	0.0
PITTSBURGH PLATE GLASS	.7294	-.0293	0.0	1.9423	-0.0996	0.0
PITTSBURGH STEEL	.5942	-.0127	0.0837	1.0621	0.0093	0.2450
POLAROID	.5000	0.0	0.0	0.6931	0.0	0.0
PORTER /H.K./	.9544	-.0051	0.0007	3.4081	-0.1181	0.0194
POTLATCH FORESTS	.9034	-.0899	0.0	2.5503	-0.5598	0.0
PROCTER & GAMBLE	.7976	0.0416	0.0	1.8834	0.1713	0.0
PULLMAN	.5954	-.0329	0.0205	1.0552	-0.0737	0.0907
QUAKER OATS	.7441	0.0368	0.0	1.7367	0.1203	0.0
RADIO CORP. OF AMERICA	.8710	0.0054	0.0120	2.2746	0.0731	0.1234
RALSTON PURINA	.4175	0.2328	0.0296	0.8108	0.6460	0.1202
RATH PACKING	.3365	0.1235	0.0	0.5193	0.1333	0.0
RAYBESTOS-MANHATTAN	.8222	-.1355	0.0	1.8415	-0.3794	0.0
RAYONIER	.3047	0.0	0.0	0.4826	0.0	0.0
RAYTHEON	.7946	-.0147	0.0576	1.7767	0.1223	0.2564
REICHHOLD CHEMICALS	.7404	-.1714	0.0646	1.5124	-0.3697	0.1970
RELIANCE ELECTRIC & ENGNG	.3698	0.2413	0.0	0.6442	0.3672	0.0
REMINGTON ARMS	.5646	0.1830	0.0	1.2165	0.4273	0.0
REPUBLIC AVIATION	.8063	0.0035	0.0	1.6804	0.1091	0.0
REPUBLIC STEEL	.4161	0.0430	0.0327	1.0704	0.0466	0.1377
REVERE COPPER & BRASS	.5637	0.0534	0.0713	1.1765	0.1872	0.3200
REVLON	.2959	-.0103	0.2617	0.6295	-0.0292	0.6304
REXALL DRUG & CHEMICAL	.7027	-.1851	0.1236	1.6966	-0.3255	0.4500
REYNOLDS METALS	.8244	-.0440	0.0081	2.0667	-0.1600	0.0680
REYNOLDS /R.J./ TOBACCO	.5000	0.0	0.3247	0.6931	0.0	1.1950
RHEEM MANUFACTURING	.7968	0.0797	0.0	2.2356	0.1791	0.0
RICHFIELD OIL	.0	0.0	0.0	0.0	0.0	0.0
RIEGEL TEXTILE	.6503	-.5215	0.0	1.2659	-0.9352	0.0
ROBERTSHAW-FULTON CONTROLS	.7157	0.0034	0.0	1.6975	0.0008	0.0
ROCKWELL MANUFACTURING	.8102	0.0267	0.0036	2.0466	0.1439	0.0375
ROCKWELL-STANDARD	.7004	-.0195	0.0	1.7568	-0.1523	0.0
ROHM & HAAS	.7609	0.0362	0.0148	1.5181	0.2176	0.1008
ROHR AIRCRAFT	.4989	-.0364	0.0	0.6921	-0.0370	0.0
ROYAL MCBEE	.6649	0.2421	0.0365	1.5359	1.2802	0.5041
RUBEROID	.8487	-.0628	0.0154	2.1161	-0.4024	0.1001
RYAN AERONAUTICAL	.7200	0.0750	0.0	1.5057	0.0911	0.0

118

Diversification: 2-Digit Groups

TABLE 5A-1 (CONT.)

COMPANY NAME	HERFINDAHL INDEX			ASH INDEX		
	1960 INDEX	CHANGE, 1960-65 OLD 2-DIGIT	NEW 2-DIGIT	1960 INDEX	CHANGE, 1960-65 OLD 2-DIGIT	NEW 2-DIGIT
ST. JOSEPH LEAD	.7731	0.0831	0.0	1.5222	0.4592	0.0
ST. REGIS PAPER	.8838	0.0018	0.0032	2.6122	-0.0671	0.0394
SCHENLEY INDUSTRIES	.5061	-.0137	0.0	0.9790	-0.0712	0.0
SCHERING	.3400	0.1979	0.0	0.6390	0.2778	0.0
SCOTT PAPER	.6876	0.0402	0.0	1.4013	0.0873	0.0
SCOVILL MANUFACTURING	.9056	-.0019	0.0074	2.6472	0.0117	0.0670
SEABOARD ALLIED MILLING	.5926	-.1309	0.0	0.9650	-0.1516	0.0
SEAGRAM /JOSEPH E./ & SONS	.5893	-.3568	0.0	1.0532	-0.6059	0.0
SHARON STEEL	.0883	0.2194	0.0507	0.2289	0.4574	0.1366
SHELL OIL	.6683	0.0400	0.0031	1.3314	0.3468	0.0245
SHERWIN-WILLIAMS	.7126	0.0855	0.0	1.7942	0.2566	0.0
SIGNAL OIL & GAS	.7376	-.2147	0.2608	1.5301	-0.7079	0.9787
SIMMONS	.7192	-.0487	0.0611	1.3235	-0.0061	0.2847
SINCLAIR OIL	.7410	0.0730	0.0108	1.6200	0.1901	0.0843
SINGER MANUFACTURING	.7827	0.1180	0.0117	1.7552	0.7686	0.1321
SKELLY OIL	.4512	-.1734	0.2847	0.6435	-0.1929	0.6229
SMITH /A.O./	.8911	-.0515	0.0094	2.5842	-0.4319	0.0742
SMITH-CORONA MARCHANT	.6963	-.1406	0.0	1.3508	-0.3587	0.0
SMITH KLINE & FRENCH LABS.	.4933	-.2847	0.2194	1.1314	-0.6283	0.5096
SOCONY MOBILE OIL	.0797	0.4462	0.1715	0.1993	0.8933	0.5205
SOUTHERN STATES COOPERATIVE	.6302	-.1340	0.0	1.0411	-0.3517	0.0
SPERRY RAND	.8911	-.0194	0.0133	2.5912	0.0275	0.0729
SPRINGS COTTON MILLS	.3788	0.2144	0.0	0.7503	0.4747	0.0
SQUARE D	.5376	0.0251	0.0	0.8601	0.1987	0.0
STALEY /A.E./ MANUFACTURING	.6332	0.0037	0.0	1.1233	0.0561	0.0
STANDARD BRANDS	.8403	0.0237	0.0	2.1605	0.0089	0.0
STANDARD KOLLSMAN	.7803	0.0299	0.0414	1.7014	0.1884	0.2871
STANDARD OIL OF CALIFORNIA	.6648	-.0409	0.0	1.4416	0.0355	0.0
STANDARD OIL /IND./	.0331	0.5003	0.0	0.1034	0.9841	0.0
STANDARD OIL /OHIO/	.2281	0.3010	0.0	0.4632	0.4430	0.0
STANDARD PACKAGING	.9187	0.0254	0.0	2.8217	0.2190	0.0
STANDARD PRESSED STEEL	.6336	-.0818	0.0	1.3238	-0.1714	0.0
STANLEY WORKS	.7663	0.0522	0.0223	1.8047	0.2755	0.1139
STAUFFER CHEMICAL	.7773	0.0047	0.0036	1.8771	0.1362	0.0316
STERLING DRUG	.7480	-.0369	0.0094	1.7424	-0.3392	0.0619
STEVENS /J.P./	.6290	0.0553	0.0094	1.0448	0.2267	0.0599
STEWART-WARNER	.9431	-.0003	0.0	3.0099	0.0548	0.0
STOKELY-VAN CAMP	.5507	-.0167	0.0728	1.1540	-0.0252	0.2023
STUDEBAKER-PACKARD	.8093	-.0087	0.0146	1.7779	-0.0272	0.1005
SUN OIL	.3750	0.1250	0.0	0.5623	0.1308	0.0

119

TABLE 5A-1 (CONT.)

COMPANY NAME	HERFINDAHL INDEX			ASH INDEX		
	1960 INDEX	CHANGE, 1960-65 OLD 2-DIGIT	NEW 2-DIGIT	1960 INDEX	CHANGE, 1960-65 OLD 2-DIGIT	NEW 2-DIGIT
SUNBEAM	.8419	-.1862	0.0675	2.0027	-0.4933	0.2696
SUNDSTRAND	.4412	-.0325	0.0	1.1428	-0.1821	0.0
SUNRAY MID-CONTINENT OIL	.5000	-.5000	0.0	0.6931	-0.6931	0.0
SUNSHINE BISCUITS	.5008	0.0235	0.0	0.8436	0.0097	0.0
SWIFT	.6317	-.0264	0.0	1.5728	-0.0494	0.0
TAPPAN	.3284	0.1059	0.2310	0.6190	0.0070	0.5867
TECUMSEH PRODUCTS	.6322	0.0083	0.0094	1.0413	0.1101	0.0558
TEXACO	.5562	-.2308	0.1679	0.9318	-0.4252	0.3514
TEXAS INSTRUMENTS	.8570	0.0263	0.0056	2.1006	0.2842	0.0607
TEXTRON	.9284	0.0291	0.0081	2.9428	0.5920	0.2215
THIOKOL CHEMICAL	.6084	-.2078	0.1086	1.1706	-0.2304	0.2892
THOMPSON RAMO WOOLDRIDGE	.9088	-.0016	0.0083	2.6629	-0.0095	0.1010
TIDEWATER OIL	.5878	0.0114	0.0	0.9696	0.0165	0.0
TIME INC.	.8586	-.0054	0.0	2.0163	0.0954	0.0
TIMES-MIRROR	.5532	0.2280	0.0309	1.2428	0.6375	0.2100
TIMKEN ROLLER BEARING	.4869	-.1519	0.0	0.7535	-0.1776	0.0
TOBIN PACKING	.0517	0.1011	0.0	0.1225	0.1643	0.0
TODD SHIPYARDS	.8904	0.0140	0.0	2.6796	0.0663	0.0
TRANE	.7639	-.0689	0.0	1.5962	-0.1748	0.0
TUNG-SOL ELECTRIC	.6564	0.0853	0.0	1.5467	-0.0063	0.0
UNDERWOOD	.5926	-.0390	0.0452	0.9650	-0.0889	0.1659
UNION BAG-CAMP PAPER	.8326	-.0049	0.0071	2.0133	-0.0030	0.0728
UNION CARBIDE	.8985	0.0253	0.0050	2.4828	0.3760	0.0946
UNION OIL OF CALIFORNIA	.4922	-.0864	0.0	0.6853	-0.0896	0.0
UNION TANK CAR	.7619	-.0218	0.0	1.7471	-0.1260	0.0
UNITED AIRCRAFT	.7062	-.0520	0.0062	1.5783	-0.1529	0.0390
UNITED BISCUIT	.0	0.0997	0.0	0.0	0.2062	0.0
UNITED MERCHANTS & MFRS.	.4277	0.0	0.0	0.6864	0.0	0.0
UNITED SHOE MACHINERY	.8965	-.0175	0.0087	2.5569	-0.0316	0.0702
U. S. GYPSUM	.6583	0.0569	0.0266	1.6712	0.1434	0.1112
U. S. INDUSTRIES	.8677	-.1038	-.0247	2.4039	-0.5913	-0.0939
U. S. PIPE & FOUNDRY	.5582	-.1358	0.0160	1.0564	-0.1896	0.0620
U. S. PLYWOOD	.6597	-.0433	0.0111	1.4220	-0.0909	0.0574
U. S. RUBBER	.7858	0.0440	0.0169	1.9460	0.2113	0.1162
U. S. STEEL	.8867	-.0022	0.0	2.6712	-0.0170	0.0
UNIVERSAL-CYCLOPS STEEL	.7280	0.0906	0.0067	1.6021	0.4027	0.0578
UNIVERSAL MATCH	.9055	-.0305	0.0139	2.6299	-0.0210	0.1291
UPJOHN	.5000	0.2816	0.0173	0.6931	0.9191	0.1116
VICK CHEMICAL	.6923	0.0695	0.0352	1.4555	0.2052	0.1590
VULCAN MATERIALS	.8624	-.0002	0.0	2.1693	0.1151	0.0

120

TABLE 5A-1 (CONT.)

COMPANY NAME	HERFINDAHL INDEX			ASH INDEX		
	1960 INDEX	CHANGE, 1960-65 OLD 2-DIGIT	NEW 2-DIGIT	1960 INDEX	CHANGE, 1960-65 OLD 2-DIGIT	NEW 2-DIGIT
WAGNER ELECTRIC	.6791	-.0004	0.0	1.1941	-0.0059	0.0
WALWORTH	.2485	-.1241	0.0	0.4964	-0.2515	0.0
WARD BAKING	.0789	0.2544	0.0	0.1715	0.5539	0.0
WARNER-LAMBERT PHARM.	.8505	-.0223	0.0107	1.9622	-0.0637	0.0858
WEST POINT MANUFACTURING	.5301	0.0437	0.0404	1.0944	0.1524	0.1395
WEST VIRGINIA PULP & PAPER	.7658	0.0494	0.0	1.6797	0.2699	0.0
WESTERN ELECTRIC	.7485	-.0719	0.0	1.5918	-0.1431	0.0
WESTERN PRINTING & LITH.	.8599	-.0003	0.0	2.0352	-0.0286	0.0
WESTINGHOUSE AIR BRAKE	.8192	-.0181	0.0278	2.0016	-0.0204	0.1270
WESTINGHOUSE ELECTRIC	.9674	0.0	0.0	3.7468	0.0261	0.0
WEYERHAEUSER	.8700	0.0	0.0068	2.1640	0.0406	0.0936
WHEELING STEEL	.4158	0.0485	0.0	0.7758	0.2461	0.0
WHIRLPOOL	.7924	0.0054	0.0021	1.6990	0.0193	0.0244
WHITE MOTOR	.2648	0.4437	0.0435	0.6125	0.8567	0.2340
WILSON	.5824	0.0623	0.0051	1.3776	0.1368	0.0324
WORTHINGTON	.8565	0.0135	0.0199	2.2212	0.0336	0.1663
WRIGLEY /WM./ JR.	.0	0.0	0.0	0.0	0.0	0.0
WYANDOTTE CHEMICALS	.8849	-.0085	0.0062	2.1796	-0.0487	0.0689
YOUNGSTOWN SHEET & TUBE	.8592	-.0184	0.0	2.0570	-0.0940	0.0
ZENITH RADIO	.7589	-.0051	0.0009	1.7336	-0.0570	0.0105

VI

Corporate Diversification and Market Structure

I N this chapter, inter-industry data for the *Fortune* corporations are aggregated: entry and exit, at the 4-digit
level, are defined as the total amount of entry and exit
registered by the *Fortune* corporations taken as a whole.
No attention is paid to the identity of any particular entering or exiting firm. The focus is entry or exit by large
corporations as a group, where large corporations are defined as the Fortune 461—the 460 *Fortune* corporations
of Chapters IV and V, plus the Hearst Corporation.

Initially, 4-digit entry and exit by these firms are related to industry characteristics that would be expected to
induce movement into or out of those industries. Is there,
for example, evidence that these large firms have responded—as might general purpose investment banks—
to particular industry characteristics in shifting resources
into or out of particular 4-digit industries as the circumstances of those industries change? If so, entry and exit
by these firms ought to show an association certainly
with the growth of those industries and perhaps also with
the size, concentration, and ease with which those industries may be entered or abandoned. If, on the other
hand, such inter-industry movements by major corporations are influenced or determined chiefly by factors
specific to the *firm*, such an overall relationship between
entry or exit and the characteristics of individual industries would not necessarily be expected. This first section

of the chapter serves therefore to illustrate the degree to which these *industry* characteristics can explain differential rates of entry and exit by the *Fortune* corporations.

The second section is more direct. Here measures of *change* in the concentration of 4-digit manufacturing industries are related to entry by these *Fortune* corporations. To what extent can entry by these large firms be shown to affect the concentration of the 4-digit industries of manufacturing—and in which direction? On the average, 4-digit industry concentration increased only very slightly during this period.[1] Nevertheless, there is opinion that increasing 4-digit concentration, where it has occurred, has been directly related to the growth and diversification of these large companies.[2] Growth by large corporations leading to increasing market concentration could, of course, occur without entry or diversification by these corporations, but a finding that concentration tends generally to fall with entry by large corporations—or a finding that this entry has been high where concentration and earnings have been high—would have quite different implications from a finding that increasing 4-digit concentration has been positively associated with 4-digit entry by these large corporations, or that such entry has been disproportionately high where concentration ratios have been low and increasing. It is to questions of this sort that this chapter is addressed.

[1] For a summary, see F. M. Scherer, *Industrial Market Structure and Economic Performance* (Chicago: Rand McNally, 1970), pp. 59-63.

[2] See, for example, William G. Shepherd, *Market Power and Economic Welfare* (New York: Random House, 1970), pp. 140-141. See also *Economic Report on Corporate Mergers*, Staff Report to the Federal Trade Commission (Government Printing Office, 1969), pp. 213-235.

DATA

The entire analysis is severely restricted by the limitations of available data. For the *Fortune* corporations, the time period involved is 1960 to 1965. Data with respect to the concentration of 4-digit manufacturing industries are not available for either year. For the 4-digit industries of manufacturing, concentration ratios are available for 1958, 1963, and 1967, but even then for only a limited (and unrepresentative) number of industries. It is possible, for example, to examine changing concentration between 1958 and 1963, and between 1958 and 1967, but for only slightly more than 200 4-digit industries in the first period and exactly 200 4-digit industries in the second.[3] In contrast, the 461 corporations considered here were active in well over 400 4-digit industries in both years for which that information is available. By necessity, the results of this chapter are based on fewer than one-half of the total number of industries than they should be. Worse than that, those industries for which data are available are those industries which are apt to be least informative.[4] The industries for which data are lacking are, for the most part, those whose definitions were altered significantly in the 1957 and subsequent revisions of the Standard Industrial Classification and would tend as a consequence to be those within which change in product composition or manufacturing process

[3] In some instances analysts have either dropped from or added to these groups. Scherer, for example, omits 29 on the grounds that industry definitions are unsatisfactory. See F. M. Scherer, *op.cit.*, p. 63. The 208 industries considered in this chapter are those for which *all* variables considered (not only concentration ratios) were available for both 1958 and 1963.

[4] See William G. Shepherd, "Trends of Concentration in American Manufacturing Industries," *Review of Economics and Statistics*, May 1964, pp. 200-212.

has been most prevalent.[5] In contrast, the 200-odd 4-digit industries for which relatively complete data are available are those which have been relatively static both with respect to product and process perhaps also with respect to market structure.

These industries are identified, together with some descriptive detail, in the appendix to this chapter. Unless otherwise noted, all data employed in this chapter are taken directly from U.S. Bureau of the Census, *Census of Manufactures*, or are built up from data provided by the 1961 and 1966 editions of the *Plant and Product Directory* prepared by *Fortune* as previously identified.

CORPORATE ENTRY AND EXIT

The rate of entry to (exit from) any 4-digit industry is usually thought to be positively (negatively) related both to anticipated earnings in that industry and to the ease with which resources may be shifted into (or out of) that industry. Under competitive conditions, entry (and exit) should tend to equalize earnings among different industries. It is widely argued that entry barriers of various sorts preclude or limit the effectiveness of this process.

However, many of the conventional barriers to entry—risk, high initial capital requirements, the need for extensive marketing networks, and so forth—are less applicable to the large corporation than to the smaller firm. Entry by large existing corporations might be viewed, therefore, as a potentially more potent regulatory force than entry by smaller corporations for whom such barriers could be more costly to overcome. The opposite or alternative view is that diversification (entry) by these

[5] See U.S. Bureau of the Budget, *Standard Industrial Classification Manual* (Washington: 1957).

125

larger corporations tends in itself to create barriers to the entry of smaller firms and thereby to reduce whatever regulatory control entry or potential entry might be able to generate.

In what follows, and as a first step, growth of industry shipments is employed as a proxy for expected industry earnings. Ease of entry is approximated (inversely) by the coverage ratio of the industry's establishments. Significant positive coefficients on these two variables, with entry as the dependent variable, would be the expected inter-industry response by these large firms. However, industry size and concentration are also introduced as independent variables. Significant negative coefficients here would suggest disproportionate expansion by large corporations to relatively small and unconcentrated industries—those industries where entry barriers of the sort indicated earlier would not be expected to be particularly important. That result would add little support for the hypothesis that increasing diversification by these large firms is a reflection of their exploitation of a comparative advantage as entrants to industries where significant entry barriers protect high earnings from the entry of smaller corporations. In each instance, exit by the *Fortune* corporations is also introduced as a dependent variable. The expectation of course is that exit should be negatively related to industry growth and positively related to ease of entry.

Two alternative measures of entry and exit are used. The specific variables employed are defined as follows:

(1) *Entry and Exit—Estimated Market Share*: Entry in this case is the estimated total employment, times 25,000, of all plants operated in the 4-digit industry in question in 1965 by firms reporting *no* plants in that industry in 1960, divided by the value of shipments of that indus-

try in 1963. On the assumption that at this time output per worker in U.S. manufacturing was roughly $25,000, this measure of entry is an approximation of the market share of industry shipments acquired by plants of the entering corporations.[6] Exit is similarly defined, except that the measure relates to plants operated in the industry in 1960 by corporations that reported no plants in the industry in 1965. Net entry is entry minus exit.

(2) *Entry and Exit—Number of Corporations*: By this measure, entry is simply the number of corporations that were not active in the industry in question in 1960 but were active in that industry in 1965, divided by the 1963 value of shipments of the industry in billions of dollars. Exit and net entry are correspondingly defined.

(3) *Industry Size*: This variable is introduced both as the natural logarithm of the industry's value of shipments in 1963 and as the 1963 value of shipments in millions of dollars.

(4) *Concentration Ratio*: This is the 4-firm concentration ratio of the 4-digit industry in 1963.

(5) *Ease of Entry*: Ease of entry is approximated by the 1963 coverage ratio of the 4-digit industry in question. The coverage ratio shows the percentage of total shipments of the industry's primary product accounted for by establishments classified within the industry.[7] It is an inverse measure of the extent to which the primary product of the industry is a secondary product of estab-

[6] For output per employee in manufacturing, see U.S. Department of Commerce, Business and Defense Services Administration, Industry Profiles, 1958-1967, Washington, D.C.: U.S. Government Printing Office, 1969. Estimated employment for plants (or portions of plants) is based on the plant weights given in the Appendix to Chapter IV. See above, p. 77.

[7] This measure is also used by Shepherd in the same context. See William G. Shepherd, *op.cit.*, p. 212.

lishments classified in other industries.[8] Where the coverage ratio is low, it is therefore probable that the primary product of that industry could readily be added by plants (or corporations) not previously active in that industry. Barriers to entry would be more likely where the coverage ratio of an industry is high, indicating that establishments classified within the industry account for the bulk of total production of the industry's primary product.

(6) *Industry Growth*: This is measured by the percentage increase in the value of shipments of the 4-digit industry from 1958 to 1963. As indicated above, this measure is interpreted as a proxy for the attractiveness of new investment in the industry. Profit measures, for 4-digit industries, are considered inadequate in this context, and are here ignored.[9] It is difficult to argue that

[8] The primary product specialization ratio—the extent to which the industry's primary product accounts for total industry shipments—is an alternative measure. Of the two, the coverage ratio would appear to be superior on *a priori* grounds. It indicates the degree to which the primary product of the industry in question is a secondary product in other industries. A relatively low primary product specialization ratio, however, need not imply that the products of establishments in the industry in question are also produced by other establishments.

[9] Profit rates for 4-digit industries are generally based on accounts for *establishments* classified within those industries. A substantial proportion of those establishments will, for the average 4-digit industry, be controlled by corporations whose activities extend beyond the 4-digit industry in question. Under these circumstances, establishment records will frequently fail to reflect accurately the contribution of those establishments to the net earnings of the parent corporation. This is the standard problem of the allocation of non-direct costs and of the accuracy of non-market determined transfer prices. Quite apart from this, there is, of course, the added problem that the average profita-

128

those industries experiencing rapid growth are not generating rates of return at the margin sufficient to support that growth, and that industries that are experiencing a decline, even a relative decline, do not offer less satisfactory earning potential. Selection of the 1958 to 1963 interval for the measurement of industry growth reflects this interpretation. Some lag in the response of corporations would be expected. The use of 1958 to 1967 as the base period does not substantially alter the regression results. Measures of industry growth for the two time periods are highly correlated.

REGRESSION RESULTS

Table 6-1 shows the results obtained when entry and exit, measured as the estimated market share of the entering and exiting firms are regressed on those independent variables indicated by the table. The table suggests that entry was significantly and negatively associated with the industry coverage ratio, and that net entry by these firms was significantly and positively associated with industry growth. Beyond that, other coefficients tend, at best, to be only marginally significant. There is slender evidence that both entry and exit are negatively associated with industry size. That association disappears with the use of net entry as the dependent variable.

The results shown in Table 6-2, where entry and exit are measured in number of companies, are similar. Once again, the coefficient on the coverage ratio is significant

---

bility of an industry may not be a good indicator of the earnings to be anticipated from additional investment in that industry. For some discussion of these and related matters, see George J. Stigler, *Capital and Rates of Return in Manufacturing Industries* (Princeton: Princeton University Press, 1963).

in the case of entry and that on industry growth significant in the case of net entry. In this table, however, the
association with the coverage ratio is significant in the
case of exit as well, and a generally higher level of significance is obtained for the coefficient on industry size.

TABLE 6-1:

REGRESSION COEFFICIENTS AND *t*-RATIOS, ENTRY, EXIT, AND NET
ENTRY BY 461 LARGE CORPORATIONS ESTIMATED MARKET
SHARE ON SELECTED INDEPENDENT VARIABLES, 1960-1965,
208 4-DIGIT INDUSTRIES[a]

Independent Variable	Entry (1)	Exit (2)	Net Entry (3)	Entry (4)	Exit (5)	Net Entry (6)
Log$_e$ Value of Shipments, 1963				-.890 (-1.75)	-2.430 (-2.66)	1.54 (1.56)
Value of Shipments, 1963 (millions of $)	-.563 (-1.43)	-.973 (-1.36)	.410 (0.54)			
Concentration Ratio, 1963	.038 (1.35)	-.003 (-0.04)	.050 (0.73)	.035 (1.28)	-.015 (-0.29)	.047 (0.91)
Coverage Ratio, 1963	-.168 (-3.45)	-.073 (0.84)	-.093 (-0.99)	-.160 (-3.36)	-.052 (-0.62)	-.107 (-1.16)
Industry Growth, 1958-1963	3.213 (1.34)	-10.079 (-2.49)	14.000 (3.01)	4.217 (1.72)	-8.030 (-1.82)	12.245 (2.57)
R^2	.09	.06	.05	.10	.06	.06

[a]The *t*-ratios are shown in parentheses.

But the most striking feature of both tables is the absence
of significant coefficients on industry concentration. There
is no evidence in either table that entry and exit by these
large corporations is at all influenced by 4-firm concentration.

That does not, however, imply that entry by these
large firms, where it has occurred, has not in itself affected the structure, or concentration, of the entered 4-
digit industries. This is the more interesting question, and

Diversification and Market Structure

William G. Shepherd has appraised the effect of increasing diversification by large corporations during roughly the same period in the following terms:

"Very broadly speaking, diversification in the United States is associated with concentration. . . . One may first

TABLE 6-2:

REGRESSION COEFFICIENTS AND t-RATIOS, ENTRY, EXIT AND NET ENTRY BY 461 LARGE CORPORATIONS (IN COMPANIES PER $1 BILLION VALUE OF SHIPMENTS) ON SELECTED INDE-PENDENT VARIABLES, 1960-1965, 208 INDUSTRIES[a]

Independent Variable	Dependent Variable					
	Entry (1)	Exit (2)	Net Entry (3)	Entry (4)	Exit (5)	Net Entry (6)
$\log_e$ Value of Shipments, 1963				-2.657 (-3.91)	-2.516 (-5.22)	-.141 (-.23)
Value of Shipments, 1963 (millions of $)	-1.052 (-1.96)	-.893 (-2.29)	-.160 (-.34)			
Concentration Ratio, 1963	.018 (.32)	.001 (.03)	.011 (.34)	-.002 (-.05)	-.013 (-.50)	.011 (.34)
Coverage Ratio, 1963	-.334 (-5.13)	-.228 (-4.80)	-.106 (-1.86)	-.313 (-4.91)	-.206 (-4.56)	-.107 (-1.86)
Industry Growth, 1958-1963	.047 (.01)	-5.89 (-2.48)	5.93 (2.07)	3.064 (.94)	-3.030 (-1.31)	6.094 (2.07)
R^2	.14	.14	.04	.19	.23	.04

[a] The t-ratios are shown in parentheses.

look at the incidence of the very largest firms in markets. In 264 product classes out of the total of 926 in 1950, at least one of the 1,000 largest firms was among the leading four producers. . . . In 1958 a majority (550) of all 1,014 product classes had a branch of at least one of the 100 largest companies among its four leading firms. But less than one-tenth (86) of the product classes had one or more such branches among its next four firms and at the same time, none in the top four. In 1963, the patterns were much the same. *Therefore, one may fairly conclude that branching by these firms tends to reinforce market*

131

power, rather than to neutralize it." (Emphasis added.)[10]

Although Shepherd's comment is worded in terms of market power, his evidence is based on aspects of market structure—the presence of large firms (or branches of large firms) among the leading firms within particular markets.[11]

But the most common measure of market structure is, of course, the 4-firm concentration ratio: the ratio of the value of shipments of the four largest firms within a given market to the total value of shipments of all firms within that market. To the extent that entry by large corporations can be shown either to reinforce, or to neutralize, market power, one place to look for that effect should also be in its impact on this measure of market structure.

A Simple Model of Structural Change

For this purpose, let VS_1^4 and VS_2^4 be the value of shipments of the four largest sellers within a given industry in the first and last years, respectively, of the time interval under consideration. Correspondingly, let VS_1 and VS_2 be the total value of shipments of the industry in those two years. The ratio of concentration in the final year to concentration in the initial year may be written as $VS_2^4/VS_2 \cdot VS_1/VS_1^4$. Consider, however, the determinants of VS_2^4. If concentration were to remain unchanged, then:

$$(1) \qquad VS_2^4 = a_0 \frac{VS_2}{VS_1} \cdot VS_1^4$$

with $a_0 = 1$ and with the four largest shippers sharing proportionately in the growth or decline of the industry.

[10] William G. Shepherd, *Market Power and Economic Welfare* (New York: Random House, 1970), pp. 140-141.

[11] *Ibid.*, pp. 143-144.

If, other things being equal, industry growth fosters increasing concentration, $a_0 > 1$; if such growth leads to decreasing concentration, $a_0 < 1$.

Now let NC_1 and NC_2 be the total number of companies present in the industry in years 1 and 2, and consider:

$$(2) \quad VS_2^4 = a_0 \left[1 + a_1 \frac{NC_2 - NC_1}{NC_2} \right] \frac{VS_2}{VS_1} \cdot VS_1^4.$$

If the number of companies is unchanged, (2) reduces to (1). The parameter a_1 in (2) simply adjusts the relationship in (1) for total entry: change in the total number of companies present. The expression is structured so that if a_1 were -1, the implication would be that the growth-adjusted value of shipments of the four largest sellers within the industry would vary in inverse proportion to the total number of companies present. That would be true if the size distribution of firms in the industry were independent of the number of firms present—if, other things being equal, a doubling of the number of firms would result in a halving of the average size of firms in each size class. If, however, the market position of leading firms were totally insulated from this overall entry, a_1 would be zero. In the unlikely event that such entry somehow facilitated growth by leading firms, a_1 would be positive.

Here, however, the issue is not this type of entry (or entry presumably by "small" corporations), but entry by corporations that are large diversifying firms. Let VS_2^E be the total value of shipments within the industry in year 2 of any such entering *large* firms, and consider

$$(3) \quad VS_2^4 = a_0 \left[1 + a_1 \frac{NC_2 - NC_1}{NC_2} \right] \frac{VS_2}{VS_1} \cdot VS_1^4 + a_2 VS_2^E.$$

133

If this entry (VS_2^E) were to reduce, on a dollar-for-dollar basis, the otherwise expected value of shipments of the leading four firms, a_2 would be -1. That would be an extreme illustration of the "creative destruction" Shepherd, for one, finds to be absent. The Shepherd thesis is that a_2 is non-negative—that "branching by these [large] firms tends to reinforce market power [$a_2 > 0$], rather than to neutralize it [$a_2 < 0$]." Any negative value of a_2 between 0 and -1 would indicate the proportion of the total market position acquired by entering *large* firms (VS_2^E) that was obtained by an equal reduction in the market position of leading firms (VS_2^4). Note that an entering large firm may become a leading firm, and hence that a positive value for a_2 is perfectly possible.

Since 4-firm concentration in year 1 ($CON4_1$) is simply VS_1^4/VS_1 and 4-firm concentration in year 2 ($CON4_2$) is VS_2^4/VS_2, (3) is readily rewritten to link changing concentration to these measures of entry in the form:

$$(4) \quad \frac{CON4_2}{CON4_1} = a_0 + a_0a_1 \frac{NC_2 - NC_1}{NC_2} + a_2 \frac{PEN}{CON4_1}$$

where $PEN = VS_2^E/VS_2$, or the market share (penetration) in year 2 of the entering large firms.

It is, however, reasonable to expect that the values of both a_1 and a_2 would be affected by the initial structure of the industry in question—for example, that:

$$(5) \quad a_1 = \beta_0 + \beta_1 CON4_1$$

and

$$(6) \quad a_2 = \lambda_0 + \lambda_1 CON4_1.$$

In the case of a_2, if concentration were very low—implying an industry in which leading firms are relatively small

—it is indeed plausible that an entering large firm would become a leading firm and that a_2 would be positive. But in terms of a "reinforcement" of market power, that case is uninteresting: there is little market power to reinforce in the first place. The interesting question is the value of $a_2 = \lambda_0 + \lambda_1 CON4_1$ where $CON4_1$ is high— where structural imperfection *is* present, and where entry by large firms *might* be capable of the competitive effect Shepherd, for example, denies.

Equally interesting is the parallel interpretation of β_0 and β_1 in the case of entry by "other" firms.[12] If the market position of leading firms is readily eroded by the entry of *any* firm, it is somewhat beside the point to worry about the entry of large firms. There ought to be enough other ("small") firms to go around. But it is entirely possible, as noted earlier, that the *important* structural imperfections arise where large leading firms in concentrated industries are able to protect by some "barrier" their market position from the competitive pressure of smaller firms—either smaller firms within the industry, or small firms that enter or attempt to enter that industry. Empirical support for this sort of hypothesis would be found in a strongly *negative* value (approaching -1) for β_0 with an offsetting *positive* value for β_1, such that $a_1 = \beta_0 + \beta_1 CON4_1 \simeq 0$ for highly concentrated industries. Under these circumstances, the value of a_2 would become doubly interesting. With evidence of leading firms being immune to the entry or penetration of

---

[12] Note that the specification of (4) a_1 relates to *all* firms, rather than all firms other than "large" firms. This specification is employed since, as indicated below, data for all companies and the number of large (*Fortune*) companies cannot be obtained for the same years.

small firms in concentrated industries, a high negative value for λ_1 would suggest competitive entry by large entering firms precisely where it is needed.

With this modification, and as fitted, (4) becomes:[13]

$$(7) \quad \frac{CON4_2}{CON4_1} = a_0 \left[1 + (\beta_0 + \beta_1 CON4_1) \frac{NC_2 - NC_1}{NC_2} \right]$$

$$+ (\lambda_0 + \lambda_1 CON4_1) \frac{PEN}{CON4_1} + \mu$$

or

$$(8) \quad \frac{CON4_2}{CON4_1} = a_0 + a_0\beta_0 \frac{NC_2 - NC_1}{NC_2} + a_0\beta_1 \frac{NC_2 - NC_1}{NC_1} \cdot CON4_1$$

$$+ \lambda_0 \frac{PEN}{CON4_1} + \lambda_1 PEN + \mu.$$

SOME EMPIRICAL RESULTS

For this purpose the variable VS_2^E is defined for each 4-digit industry as the total estimated employment, times $25,000, of those plants (among all plants reported by the 461 *Fortune* corporations) entering the industry between 1960 and 1965. The $25,000 is an approximation of output per worker in manufacturing establishments.[14] The variable *PEN* is this measure of entry by large cor-

[13] Note that the identical regression coefficients with a much higher R^2 could be obtained by fitting the form of equation (3). The form fitted uses change in concentration as the dependent variable, thereby normalizing by the variable that would be most effective in reducing unexplained variance.

Note also that if (5) and (6) are considered stochastic, this specification is obviously heteroscedastic. Correction is not readily feasible. See H. Theil, *Principles of Econometrics* (New York, John Wiley and Sons, 1971), pp. 622-627.

[14] See above, footnote 6.

porations (VS_2^E) divided by the value of shipments in the industry in 1963 and is therefore the estimated market share (penetration) of the entering corporations.[15] Other variables in the model are value of shipments, number of companies, and 4-firm concentration by 4-digit industries. These measures are available from the Census of Manufacturers for 1958, 1963, and 1967.[16] As noted earlier, it was possible to assemble all variables in each year for 200 4-digit industries. Since the Census years do not match those for which the large corporate entry variable can be defined, Table 6-3 shows regression results for change in concentration over the three alternative time periods: 1958 to 1967, 1958 to 1963, and 1963 to 1967. Parameters are defined in the table with the notation introduced earlier. In each case, the measure of large firm entry (*PEN*) is the same. All other variables are specific to the time period indicated. In each case as well, the fit is to observations for the same 200 4-digit industries.[17]

[15] Note that the *Fortune* data do not identify plants acquired by merger, and that *measure of entry includes "entry" by merger.* It is not possible with these data, or with any other such data for this period, to distinguish entry by merger from entry resulting from the creation of new facilities without any form of corporate acquisition.

[16] *Concentration Ratios in Manufacturing Industry, 1967.* Report prepared by the Bureau of the Census for the Subcommittee on Antitrust and Monopoly of the Committee on the Judiciary of the United States Senate (Government Printing Office, 1971).

[17] The parameters of interest in (8) above—e.g., the vector $\theta = (a_0, \beta_0, \beta_1, \lambda_0, \lambda_1)$—can be estimated either by ordinary least squares or by nonlinear techniques. Point estimates will be identical in the two cases. However, nonlinear techniques permit calculation of standard errors for all components of θ, whereas with the specification of (8) ordinary least squares does not.

In Table 6-3, $\hat{a}_0$ is generally close to the expected (neutral) value of 1.0 and $\hat{\beta}_0$ is negative, again as expected. However, $\hat{\beta}_1$ is strongly positive: as concentration increases, the concentration-reducing effect of total entry

TABLE 6-3:

REGRESSION COEFFICIENTS AND *t*-RATIOS: CHANGE IN 4-FIRM
CONCENTRATION, 1958-1967, 1958-1963 AND 1963-1967,
REGRESSED ON SELECTION INDEPENDENT VARIABLES,
200 4-DIGIT MANUFACTURING INDUSTRIES[a]

| Regression | Time Period | | |
Coefficient	1958-1967	1958-1963	1963-1967
$\hat{a}_0$	1.067	1.047	1.031
	(39.64)	(57.65)	(80.67)
$\hat{\beta}_0$	-.745	-.539	-.671
	(-5.22)	(-3.22)	(-4.97)
$\hat{\beta}_1$	1.067	.722	.966
	(3.63)	(2.11)	(3.68)
$\hat{\lambda}_0$	.526	.351	.093
	(4.15)	(3.91)	(1.43)
$\hat{\lambda}_1$	-1.670	-1.071	-.433
	(-4.25)	(-3.86)	(-2.19)
R^2	.24	.14	.17

[a] See text, equation (8) and footnote 17. The numbers in parentheses are *t*-ratios.

Appropriate variances and covariances were therefore obtained by inverting

$$R = \frac{1}{2\hat{\sigma}^2}\left[\frac{\partial^2 S}{\partial\theta\partial\theta'}\right]$$

where $\hat{\sigma}^2$ is the estimated residual variance and S the sum of squares. This is the equivalent of using the Cramer-Rao bound in the context maximum likelihood estimation. See S. M. Goldfeld and R. E. Quandt, *Nonlinear Methods in Econometrics* (North Holland, 1972), Chapter 2.

decreases. The effect of entry by large firms, however, is almost exactly the opposite: $\hat{\lambda}_0$ is *positive.* When concentration is low, $\hat{a}_2 \simeq \hat{\lambda}_0$ and the effect of entry by large firms, other things being equal, is projected as an *increase* in concentration. But $\hat{\lambda}_1$ is strongly negative. As initial concentration is increased, therefore, $\hat{a}_2$ also becomes negative. For convenience, Table 6-4 contains the values of $\hat{a}_1 = \hat{\beta}_0 + \hat{\beta}_1 CON4_1$ and of $\hat{a}_2 = \hat{\lambda}_0 + \hat{\lambda}_1 CON4_1$ im-

TABLE 6-4:

CALCULATED VALUES[a] OF $\hat{a}_1 = \hat{\beta}_0 + \hat{\beta}_1 CON4_1$ AND OF $\hat{a}_2 = \hat{\lambda}_0 + \hat{\lambda}_1 CON4_1$ FOR ILLUSTRATIVE VALUES OF $CON4_1$

| | Time Period | | | | | |
| | 1958-1967 | | 1958-1963 | | 1963-1967 | |
$CON4_1$	$\hat{a}_1$	$\hat{a}_2$	$\hat{a}_1$	$\hat{a}_2$	$\hat{a}_1$	$\hat{a}_2$
.25	-.476	.109	-.359	.083	-.430	-.015
	(-5.64)	(1.41)	(-3.78)	(1.52)	(-5.39)	(-0.40)
.40	-.314	-.142	-.250	-.078	-.285	-.080
	(-4.73)	(-1.48)	(-3.70)	(-1.16)	(-4.89)	(-1.76)
.60	-.099	-.476	-.106	-.293	-.092	-.166
	(-1.19)	(-3.06)	(-1.27)	(-2.67)	(-1.41)	(-2.21)
.75	.062	-.725	.002	-.453	.053	-.231
	(0.53)	(-3.48)	(0.02)	(-3.08)	(0.57)	(-2.27)

[a] The numbers in parentheses are *t*-ratios. Note that, strictly speaking, these estimates are not distributed as *t*. See text, footnote 18.

plied for different levels of concentration by the regression coefficients of Table 6-3.[18] Table 6-4 shows the clear

[18] Standard errors for $\hat{a}_1$ and $\hat{a}_2$ were calculated from the variance-covariance matrices for the parameters of θ. See above, footnote 15. As a check on the accuracy of this procedure, exact confidence intervals for $\hat{a}_1$ were also calculated by solving the quadratic in a_1 of:

$$(\hat{a}_0 a_1 - \widehat{a_0 \beta_0} - \widehat{a_0 \beta_1} CON4_1)^2 = t^2 s_z^2$$

where $z = \hat{a}_0 - \widehat{a_0 \beta_0} - \widehat{a_0 \beta_1} CON4_1$, *t* is the appropriate *t* sta-

tendency for the estimated effect of entry by large firms on 4-firm concentration ($\hat{a}_2$) to become strongly negative as the level of concentration increases. It also shows the reverse tendency for the calculated value of $\hat{a}_1$ (the coefficient on total or "small" firm entry) to approach zero as concentration increases. Those results clearly suggest that where concentration is high, the market position of leading firms tends to be protected from erosion through the entry of "small" firms ($\hat{a}_1$). But the case of entry by large firms ($\hat{a}_2$) is the reverse. Furthermore, the estimated value of $\hat{a}_2$ is such that the projected impact of entry to concentrated industries by large firms is not small. A coefficient of $-.7$ implies, for example, that 70 percent of the market share of entering large firms is acquired at the expense of the leading four firms.

CHANGING 8-FIRM CONCENTRATION

Tables 6-5 and 6-6 show very similar results for change in 8-firm concentration. Here the fitted form is

$$(9) \quad \frac{CON8_2}{CON8_1} = a_0 + a_0\beta_0 \frac{NC_2 - NC_1}{NC_2} + a_0\beta_1 \frac{NC_2 - NC_1}{NC_2} \cdot CON8_1$$

$$+ \lambda_0 \frac{PEN}{CON8_1} + \lambda_1 PEN + \mu$$

where $CON8$ is the 8-firm concentration ratio with, as

---

tistic, and s_z^2 is the estimated variance of z. Variances and covariances for $\hat{a}_0$, $\widehat{a_0\beta_0}$ and $\widehat{a_0\beta_1}$ were in this case estimated by ordinary least squares. With t set at 1.96, virtually identical confidence intervals were obtained with the two methods. For a similar application of this technique, which is an old one, see Zvi Griliches, "Distributed Lags: A Survey," *Econometrica*, January 1967, pp. 32-33.

before, the subscripts indicating the initial or the terminal year of the time period in question.[19]

Some differences are to be expected. For example, the estimated coefficient $\hat{\lambda}_0$ is larger for change in 8-firm concentration than for change in 4-firm concentration: where concentration is low, it is *a priori* more likely that

TABLE 6-5:

REGRESSION COEFFICIENTS AND *t*-RATIOS: CHANGE IN 8-FIRM CONCENTRATION, 1958-1967, 1958-1963 AND 1963-1967, REGRESSED ON SELECTED INDEPENDENT VARIABLES, 200 4-DIGIT MANUFACTURING INDUSTRIES[a]

Regression Coefficient	Time Period		
	1958-1967	1958-1963	1963-1967
$\hat{a}_0$	1.054	1.038	1.022
	(53.89)	(77.03)	(111.99)
$\hat{\beta}_0$	-.668	-.528	-.735
	(-5.69)	(-3.62)	(-6.55)
$\hat{\beta}_1$	.744	.550	.876
	(3.89)	(2.42)	(5.13)
$\hat{\lambda}_0$	.727	.237	.242
	(4.74)	(3.56)	(3.21)
$\hat{\lambda}_1$	-1.571	-.790	-.523
	(-4.86)	(-3.85)	(-3.32)
R^2	.28	.15	.27

[a] See text, equation (9) and footnote 17. The numbers in parentheses are *t*-ratios.

an entering large firm would displace one of the eight leading firms than one of the top four. That is what the comparison indicates. Similarly, the estimated coefficient

[19] As with (8), standard errors for the parameters of interest were obtained through nonlinear estimation. See above, footnote 15.

$\hat{\beta}_1$ is lower in Table 6-5 than in Table 6-3: where concentration is high, it is (perhaps) more likely that entry by "small" firms would reduce the market share of the leading eight than that of the leading four. Even these differences, however, are readily exaggerated: 8-firm concentration will always exceed 4-firm concentration. Taking

TABLE 6-6:

CALCULATED VALUES[a] OF $\hat{a}_1 = \hat{\beta}_0 + \hat{\beta}_1 CON8_1$ AND FOR $\hat{a}_2 = \hat{\lambda}_0 + \hat{\lambda}_1 CON8_1$ FOR ILLUSTRATIVE VALUES OF $CON8_1$

| | Time Period | | | | | |
| | 1958-1967 | | 1958-1963 | | 1963-1967 | |
$CON8_1$	$\hat{a}_1$	$\hat{a}_2$	$\hat{a}_1$	$\hat{a}_2$	$\hat{a}_1$	$\hat{a}_2$
.25	-.482	.333	-.391	.040	-.516	.109
	(-6.31)	(3.49)	(-4.14)	(0.99)	(-6.98)	(2.39)
.40	-.370	.098	-.308	-.079	-.385	.029
	(-6.48)	(1.19)	(-4.56)	(-1.58)	(-7.10)	(0.76)
.60	-.221	-.216	-.199	-.237	-.210	-.078
	(-4.51)	(-2.06)	(-4.03)	(-2.92)	(-5.25)	(-1.57)
.75	-.110	-.451	-.115	-.355	-.078	-.157
	(-1.81)	(-3.23)	(-1.95)	(-3.26)	(-1.70)	(-2.34)

[a] The numbers in parentheses are *t*-ratios. See text, footnote 18.

that into account, the two sets of results are remarkably consistent, although they are of course scarcely independent. Nevertheless, repeating the test with market shares of the eight leading firms does not alter the general conclusion: entry by these 461 large firms during this period does *not* appear by this test to have been a factor tending to increase concentration. The implication of these data for concentrated industries is just the reverse.

It is certainly appropriate at this point to note that Shepherd conditioned his earlier comment, and his use of the very limited data available, with the observation: "Accurate and full evidence . . . would not be difficult for the Census Bureau to compute, and it would go far to clarify the real causes and effects of diversification."[20] That is also the conclusion here. Given the very crude measures of diversifying activity employed here, that the results reported are as consistent as they are is (1) remarkable and (2) as a result also illustrative of the need for those more accurate and hopefully more revealing Census tabulations.

SUMMARY

This chapter examines the inter-industry movement of 461 large industrial corporations among some 200 4-digit industries for which data can be assembled during the early 1960's. At the outset, the chapter looks for evidence that entry and exit by these large firms has been related to particular characteristics of those 4-digit industries. The evidence is sketchy. There is a relationship between industry growth and net entry, as defined above, by these large corporations; but the relationship is not strong. If entry and exit are taken independently, the significance of even that relationship disappears. The most robust result is that entry is higher, other things being equal, in industries where the coverage ratio is low. That is an expected result and scarcely a major one. On the whole, the data manipulated in this fashion fail to show much at all regarding the determination of the rate of entry and exit by these large firms.

That, however, is not the case when the share of the four or eight largest firms in 4-digit industries is examined in the context of entry by these *Fortune* firms. There is a *negative* association between change in the share of the four (or eight) largest sellers in concentrated industries

---

[20] William G. Shepherd, *op.cit.*, p. 140.

and entry by large firms. Not only that, but the regression results suggest the mirror image in the case of entry by small firms: where concentration is high, entry by small firms appears to make no significant effect on a reduction in industry concentration.

That is the most worrisome (and perhaps also the most interesting) result—relatively strong evidence that the market position of leading firms *is* protected in concentrated industries from entry by other than large firms.

Some of the implications of all this are developed in the following chapter. The Appendix to this chapter provides additional detail with respect to the processing of the *Fortune* data and the measures of entry and exit that underlie this analysis. Appendix Table 6A-1 contains the measures themselves.

Appendix

The following table lists the number of the 461 *Fortune* corporations active in each of 208 4-digit industries in 1960. Entry and exit by the *Fortune* corporations between 1960 and 1965 are also shown. The 208 4-digit are those on which regression results of Tables 6-1 and 6-2 are based. The first 200 are those for which it was possible to assemble appropriate data for the 1958 to 1967 interval, and are the industries on which the results of Tables 6-3 through 6-8 are based.

Entry and exist are shown both as the number of entering and exiting companies and as plant employment (times 25,000) divided by the 1963 value of shipments of the industry. These latter measures, indicated by *PEN* and *PEXT* in the table, are crude approximations of the total market share of the entering and exiting firms. See above, pp. 137. In a number of instances, those approximations are clearly implausible. For an extreme example, in the case of 4-digit industry 2097 (manufactured ice) two exiting corporations are shown to account for 1.8 times total shipments of the industry. Error of this sort can arise in a number of ways. As noted in the appendix to Chapter III, the estimated employment of multi-product plants is split equally among all 4-digit products. The importance of relatively minor products (manufactured ice?) is apt to be overestimated by this procedure. Also as noted in Chapter III, where the employment of an individual establishment is unknown, it is estimated as having average employment. That would also tend to inflate the estimated importance of products typically

145

produced by relatively small plants. Finally, the use of $25,000 as an across-the-board measure of output per employee undoubtedly introduces distortion. Rather than attempt to identify and remove subjectively such "implausible" estimates, this chapter reports results for all industries for which data could be assembled. The basic *Fortune* data are shown below.

Diversification and Market Structure

TABLE 6A-1:

SELECTED DESCRIPTIVE DETAIL: 208 4-DIGIT INDUSTRIES;
461 *Fortune* CORPORATIONS

Industry Code	No. of "Fortune" Companies 1960	Entry by "Fortune" Companies 1960-1965		Exit by "Fortune" Companies 1960-1965	
		Number	PEN[a]	Number	PEXT[b]
2011	12	1	.003	1	.001
2021	11	1	.005	1	.012
2024	10	2	.012	1	.001
2026	10	–	–	–	–
2034	7	6	.133	1	.002
2036	1	2	.032	1	.013
2041	10	–	–	–	–
2042	35	10	.048	8	.031
2043	9	2	.005	–	–
2044	1	1	.005	–	–
2046	8	4	.076	–	–
2051	9	3	.014	–	–
2063	1	1	.036	–	–
2071	11	6	.072	1	.009
2072	2	2	.092	–	–
2073	2	2	.077	–	–
2082	3	–	–	–	–
2083	2	3	.199	–	–
2084	2	2	.151	–	–
2085	5	–	–	–	–
2086	4	3	.004	1	.007
2087	9	4	.010	1	.006
2091	6	–	–	2	.007
2092	16	1	.001	5	.015
2093	8	3	.166	3	.143
2096	12	2	.003	2	.009
2097	3	1	.042	2	1.861
2098	2	3	.047	2	.020
2121	2	1	.037	–	–
2131	5	–	–	–	–
2141	–	1	.001	–	–
2241	6	4	.044	1	.004
2253	4	–	–	3	.037
2254	1	–	–	–	–
2256	5	4	.105	–	–
2259	1	–	–	–	–

147

TABLE 6A-1 (*cont.*)

Industry Code	No. of "Fortune" Companies 1960	Entry by "Fortune" Companies 1960-1965		Exit by "Fortune" Companies 1960-1965	
		Number	PEN[a]	Number	PEXT[b]
2284	1	–	–	–	–
2291	3	–	–	1	.112
2292	–	–	–	–	–
2293	4	–	–	1	.085
2294	4	–	–	1	.229
2295	10	6	.172	1	.006
2297	1	–	–	–	–
2298	5	1	.089	1	.089
2311	3	3	.092	–	–
2321	5	–	–	2	.004
2322	4	1	.033	2	.040
2323	1	–	–	1	.082
2327	4	2	.014	–	–
2331	2	2	.059	1	.003
2337	1	4	.015	–	–
2341	4	1	.014	–	–
2342	2	–	–	–	–
2363	1	–	–	1	.010
2381	2	–	–	1	.234
2385	1	1	4.67	–	–
2386	–	–	–	–	–
2387	1	–	–	–	–
2391	–	–	–	–	–
2393	2	1	.061	1	.025
2394	2	1	.034	2	.039
2433	3	8	.209	1	.022
2443	1	1	.179	–	–
2445	4	–	–	–	–
2491	6	–	–	2	.061
2511	12	6	.039	3	.015
2514	7	4	.053	4	.042
2519	3	3	.239	2	.248
2521	2	5	.185	2	.424
2522	3	2	.018	1	.003
2531	5	4	.051	2	.011
2591	1	1	.008	1	.007
2611	20	3	.131	1	.008
2642	4	3	.051	–	–
2644	2	1	.023	1	.301

TABLE 6A-1 *(cont.)*

Industry Code	No. of "Fortune" Companies 1960	Entry by "Fortune" Companies 1960-1965		Exit by "Fortune" Companies 1960-1965	
		Number	PEN[a]	Number	PEXT[b]
2646	7	–	–	–	–
2711	3	–	–	–	–
2721	7	–	–	1	.007
2731	5	–	–	–	–
2732	3	4	.063	1	.003
2741	5	2	.053	–	–
2753	6	2	.104	2	.020
2771	3	–	–	–	–
2789	1	1	.011	1	.022
2791	–	–	–	–	–
2793	3	–	–	1	.007
2794	2	–	–	1	.020
2812	21	3	.034	4	.049
2813	17	11	.125	1	.039
2816	17	7	.104	6	.065
2818	73	20	.022	10	.032
2822	15	5	.029	3	.013
2831	14	5	.326	2	.248
2833	24	8	.199	6	.273
2834	24	4	.007	3	.006
2844	15	7	.020	3	.006
2871	15	9	.289	5	.275
2872	11	6	.120	5	.118
2892	8	2	.034	–	–
2893	10	4	.152	3	.190
2911	42	2	.001	8	.005
2951	14	3	.082	2	.047
2952	15	2	.022	2	.014
2992	14	4	.022	3	.009
2999	9	2	.056	5	.673
3021	4	–	–	–	–
3111	5	–	–	1	.020
3121	2	–	–	1	.284
3131	8	2	.015	4	.138
3141	9	–	–	–	–
3142	3	–	–	1	.081
3199	3	1	.025	1	.082
3221	7	–	–	–	–
3229	9	2	.107	1	.008

TABLE 6A-1 *(cont.)*

Industry Code	No. of "Fortune" Companies 1960	Entry by "Fortune" Companies 1960-1965		Exit by "Fortune" Companies 1960-1965	
		Number	PEN[a]	Number	PEXT[b]
3241	11	–	–	1	.001
3251	2	2	.051	1	.130
3255	5	3	.043	–	–
3261	4	–	–	–	–
3262	–	1	.029	–	–
3263	–	–	–	–	–
3264	11	1	.011	1	.019
3273	9	2	.002	4	.011
3274	12	2	.092	3	.047
3275	10	3	.102	1	.001
3281	–	1	.042	–	–
3292	16	3	.098	3	.028
3293	10	1	.002	1	.008
3313	13	3	.074	4	.143
3321	25	12	.079	2	.003
3322	11	2	.116	4	.043
3323	24	3	.062	3	.025
3341	11	7	.058	3	.020
3356	15	7	.093	4	.022
3391	20	2	.007	3	.019
3411	12	5	.059	1	.001
3421	5	2	.046	–	–
3425	3	–	–	1	.036
3444	20	9	.059	5	.022
3451	9	1	.004	2	.007
3452	20	6	.029	2	.010
3481	14	5	.014	6	.020
3494	36	14	.066	10	.024
3496	2	1	.064	–	–
3498	10	4	.073	7	.125
3499	34	15	.167	12	.094
3534	4	1	.009	–	–
3537	11	7	.260	4	.183
3541	19	5	.021	4	.025
3551	15	8	.061	2	.001
3552	6	5	.062	3	.006
3553	10	2	.072	4	.043
3554	14	2	.024	3	.038
3555	6	11	.206	2	.015

TABLE 6A-1 (*cont.*)

Industry Code	No. of "Fortune" Companies 1960	Entry by "Fortune" Companies 1960-1965		Exit by "Fortune" Companies 1960-1965	
		Number	PEN[a]	Number	PEXT[b]
3562	8	4	.099	–	–
3564	15	6	.324	1	.017
3572	7	–	–	1	.042
3582	4	4	.712	3	.156
3586	3	–	–	–	–
3612	13	3	.012	1	.018
3621	32	12	.035	4	.040
3623	9	8	.194	1	.009
3624	5	3	.044	1	.029
3633	10	5	.047	2	.021
3641	7	1	.002	2	.032
3642	16	4	.117	1	.001
3652	2	1	.028	1	.008
3691	5	2	.013	1	.011
3692	4	2	.094	–	–
3693	8	3	.345	2	.026
3694	15	7	.035	5	.056
3713	6	2	.052	1	.005
3715	5	3	.143	1	.003
3721	26	5	.050	5	.065
3722	30	16	.082	9	.015
3731	8	4	.047	2	.003
3732	7	5	.174	2	.089
3741	7	4	.233	4	.078
3742	12	6	.045	1	.002
3751	4	1	.003	–	–
3831	12	6	.094	3	.042
3843	2	–	–	–	–
3851	3	1	.008	–	–
3861	17	3	.005	4	.023
3871	6	6	.138	2	.008
3872	–	–	–	–	–
3911	–	–	–	–	–
3912	–	–	–	–	–
3914	3	–	–	2	.158
3941	4	1	.003	2	.028
3943	2	–	–	2	.271
3949	12	3	.069	3	.027
3952	1	–	–	1	.041

Diversification and Market Structure

TABLE 6A-1 (cont.)

Industry Code	No. of "Fortune" Companies 1960	Entry by "Fortune" Companies 1960-1965		Exit by "Fortune" Companies 1960-1965	
		Number	PEN[a]	Number	PEXT[b]
3953	2	–	–	1	.013
3955	8	3	.253	1	.032
3961	2	1	.039	–	–
3963	–	1	.134	–	–
3964	2	1	.003	–	–
3981	12	3	.048	6	.124
3988	–	1	.017	–	–
3993	2	4	.069	1	.004
2094	10	39	.078	3	.044
2815	26	8	.088	2	.104
2819	75	18	.052	14	.005
3423	13	7	.028	2	.019
3461	40	10	.026	8	.001
3982	3	2	.029	–	–
3983	3	–	–	–	–
3995	–	–	–	–	–

[a]PEN is defined as in the text to this chapter and is the estimated plant employment in 1965 of all entering corporations multiplied by 25,000 and divided by the value of shipments of the industry in 1963.

[b]PEXT is the estimated plant employment in 1960 of all exiting corporations multiplied by 25,000 and divided by the value of shipments of the industry in 1963.

VII

Summary and Interpretation

O NE commonly held opinion is that an important
component of relative growth by large corporations
is increasing diversification by the most rapidly growing
corporations.[1] A second is that this growth and diversification has generally worsened the structure of industrial
markets.[2] These are the aspects of large-scale corporate
growth to which this study is directed. It should be clear
that it is not concerned with any political question of the
social power, influence, or behavior of corporate bigness.
It is concerned with industrial diversification as a source
of corporate growth and of *economic* power.

QUESTIONS

In that context, it asks four questions. First, is there valid
empirical evidence of a relationship between corporate
growth and diversification? For all large firms, taken as a

---

[1] See, for example, Study Paper Number Two, of the *Studies
by the Staff of the Cabinet Committee on Price Stability*, which
notes: "The result has been the creation of many vast enter-
prises cutting across a broad array of industries. As shown above,
the 200 largest corporations have expanded greatly the number of industries in which they participate." See *Studies by the
Staff of the Cabinet Committee on Price Stability* (Washington:
January 1969), p. 81.

[2] Shepherd, for example, concludes that diversification by these
firms tends to reinforce market power rather than to neutralize
it. See William G. Shepherd, *Market Power and Economic Welfare* (New York: Random House, 1970), pp. 140-141.

153

group, can such a relationship be identified? Second, is there evidence in any such relationship of a tendency for growth-related diversification to be among potentially or actively competing 4-digit industries? How diverse has been that diversification that has led to or been accompanied by relatively rapid growth?[3] Third, can it be demonstrated that entry by large corporations to new markets has been related to the structural characteristics of those markets, and what, if any, is the nature of that relationship?[4] Fourth, is there evidence that entry to new markets by large corporations has in general been accompanied by increasing (or for that matter decreasing) concentration within those markets? The period under consideration is the late 1950's and early 1960's. The answers are mixed.

GROWTH AND DIVERSIFICATION

Those of the 500 largest industrial corporations in 1960 which survived to 1965 as independent entities did diversify during this period. On the average, however, that diversification, especially given the wide range in the initial diversification of these corporations, was not great. Interestingly, the most diversified, by the definition of diversification employed here, were corporations such as General Electric and Westinghouse.[5]

Probably more significant than this increase in diversification, particularly as an indicator of the future struc-

---

[3] This question is introduced in Chapter IV. Additional measures of 4-digit diversification are developed in Chapter V. The analysis of that chapter is specifically concerned with this issue.

[4] Primary characteristics considered are industry size, concentration, coverage, and growth, all at the 4-digit industry level. See Chapter VI, pp. 126 to 128.

[5] For a list of diversification indices for the large firms considered, see Chapter IV, Appendix, Table 4A-1.

ture of industry, is the much larger increase in the number of products reported by these firms between 1960 and 1965[6]—probably, because the evidence is partially contradictory. In terms of growth-related activity, entry serves as a slightly better explanatory variable for corporate growth than does increasing diversification. At the same time, there is, in the stability of the diversification indices themselves, the suggestion that much of that entry reflects the addition of products representing very little of the total productive activity of the firms in question.[7]

Nevertheless, there *is* evidence during this period that increasing diversification was related to the growth of large firms. But there is much stronger evidence, in a similar setting, that corporate earnings were a more important factor in relative growth within this population of the largest industrial corporations.[8] There is also at least the suggestion that the causality in this analysis may be reversed. Large firms tend to be diversified firms. Firms with high earnings tend to grow. Growing firms tend therefore to diversify. That argument is equally applicable to entry, which shows much the same kind of relationship, although a slightly stronger one, with the growth rates displayed by these large companies.

The causality, however, is not critical. If growing firms diversify, then growing firms—for whatever reason—find it advantageous to diversify. Diversification therefore contributes to that growth. Without diversification, growth would be more difficult. More important is the nature of the diversification and entry that underlie—or, if you like, accompany—that growth.

[6] See Chapter IV, Table 4-1.
[7] See Chapter IV, Table 4-3.
[8] See Chapter IV, pp. 70 and 71.

Available measures of diversification and of changing diversification are based on the Standard Industrial Classification. But different S.I.C. categories can represent closely related—in an economic sense—industries, or totally unrelated ones. Increasing diversification may therefore combine within the same firm closely related (and potentially or actively competing) productive activity or, alternatively, activities that are totally unrelated one from another in terms of the economic markets involved. Determination of which is which, is not easy. Chapter V employs the 2-digit Standard Industrial Classification to differentiate between "related" and "unrelated" 4-digit industries.[9]

On that basis, there is no clear evidence that diversification leading to (or accompanying) relatively rapid corporate growth has been primarily among related 4-digit industries. Increasing 4-digit diversification *within* 2-digit industry groups is approximately as growth-related in these data as is increasing 4-digit diversification *across* 2-digit industry groups.

The finding is a negative one. The data fail to show a differential effect between the two categories of changing diversification (and corresponding measures of 4-digit entry) for these 460 corporations. But the data also fail to show much in the way of regularity when the inter-industry activity of these corporations is related to the characteristics of individual 4-digit industries within manufacturing. If diversification is not a response to the present (favorable) position of particular (growing) firms, then the inter-industry activity of these firms ought to show a response to the growth and decline of individual

[9] Related 4-digit industries are considered to be those classified within the same 2-digit industry group. See Chapter V, pp. 91 to 94.

industries. It does, but the level of explanation achieved in this manner is very low.

CHANGING 4-DIGIT CONCENTRATION

Much more important, however: these data provide no support for the proposition that entry by these large corporations tended to result in increased 4-firm 4-digit concentration. Indeed, they suggest the opposite.[10] Where concentration was initially high, the rate of entry by firms among this group of large corporations was positively and significantly associated with decreasing 4-firm 4-digit concentration. That, of course, does not imply that, where concentration ratios have been rising, expansion by firms among the largest cannot have been responsible. Neither does it indicate that if, for example, 20-firm concentration ratios had been employed similar results would have been forthcoming. But the data absolutely fail to support the contention that inter-industry activity by these large firms during this period led to increasing 4- or 8-firm concentration in already concentrated 4-digit industries. They show the reverse, and about that there is no question.

SOME IMPLICATIONS

A central thought throughout this work is that the growth and industrial diversification of large corporations can be either beneficial or detrimental to the functioning of industrial markets.[11] In such markets structural imperfection rests largely, if not entirely, on the presence of some sort of barrier to the entry of potentially competing

[10] See Chapter VI, esp. pp. 132 to 142.

[11] This argument is also developed in Charles H. Berry, "Corporate Bigness and Diversification in Manufacturing," *Ohio State Law Journal*, Vol. 28, No. 3, Summer 1967.

firms. Apart from legislated barriers—patents and licenses and the like—the more important barriers can be traced, in one way or another, to questions of size, and increasingly to the advantages of corporate size. Under such circumstances, it is reasonable to expect that when significant entry occurs, or where the threat of entry is real, it will frequently, or even generally, involve large corporations—corporations of the size of those considered in the preceding analysis.[12]

That entry can be competitive, but it can also be anti-competitive. For example, it is simply not true, as is sometimes argued, that "conglomerate" expansion is not a way of creating monopoly power.[13] It can be, and it will be, if it involves the acquisition of actively or potentially competing facilities. It will not be if the markets involved are independent. It is for precisely this reason

[12] It is this aspect of industrial organization that underlies, presumably, the conclusion of the Task Force on Antitrust Policy: "Our proposal focuses on the second probability, that a substantial number of large diversified firms will enter a substantial number of concentrated industries, and is intended to channel the potential competition of large firms along lines that are conducive to reducing levels of concentration in the American economy." *Task Force Report on Antitrust Policy* (Washington: May 21, 1969), p. iii-13.

[13] For a contrary view, see the statement by Robert Bork in *Task Force Report on Antitrust Policy, op.cit.*, pp. 3-A to 5-A. Note, however, that the argument is largely semantic. If, by definition, a conglomerate expansion always involves acquisition of facilities in *totally* unrelated industries, then Bork is quite correct. But that is not the way conglomerate mergers are always defined. Under the heading of conglomerate mergers, the Federal Trade Commission includes "geographic market extension mergers"—the merger of corporations that manufacture the *same* industry but sell in different parts of the country. See Federal Trade Commission, *Economic Report on Corporate Mergers* (Washington: 1969), p. 59.

that the preceding analysis attempts to distinguish 4-digit diversification that is within 2-digit industry groups from that which is among such 2-digit categories.[14] The data fail to show that corporate growth has responded chiefly to 4-digit diversification that is within rather than among digit industry groups. But measure of market interdependence is far from perfect. It would be exceedingly interesting to determine if a more detailed classification of "related" industries would also generate a similar finding.[15] Nevertheless, that finding is consistent with the rather striking conclusion of Chapter VI: entry by these large corporations to concentrated industries appears to have contributed, other things being equal and during this time period, to a reduction in the relative size of leading firms within those entered industries. It is in exactly that same setting—in concentrated industries—that Chapter VI also shows empirical evidence that leading firms tend to be relatively isolated from the competitive pressure of entering smaller firms. The implication is that at least some share of the inter-industry activity—diversification —by these large firms contributed toward the creation of improved market structure precisely where it was most needed.

The Question of Mergers

Diversification by large firms will generally be accomplished by merger. The measures of entry and changing

[14] The same distinction is employed by the Federal Trade Commission. See *Economic Report on Corporate Mergers*, Staff Report to the Federal Trade Commission (Government Printing Office, 1969), pp. 242-247.

[15] Such a classification is also proposed, but far from accomplished, by Narver. See J. Narver, *Conglomerate Mergers and Market Competition* (Berkeley: University of California Press, 1967).

diversification developed here for the 460-461 firms are undoubtedly a reflection of merger activity. From the data available, the extent to which mergers account for this inter-industry expansion simply cannot be determined. But for large firms—and these are large firms—the conventional route to entry or diversification is the corporate acquisition or merger.[16] It seems likely that much of what is here recorded is the impact of merger activity, not the *de novo* creation of new manufacturing facilities.

While the preceding findings are in general reassuring rather than alarming, they do not suggest that policy concern with corporate growth and diversification by merger is misplaced at the present time. What they do suggest is an attitude towards it.[17] The problem, of course, is that diversification by merger results only in a different competitor within the entered market, not a new competitor. The regulatory impact of that kind of entry depends therefore only on the behavioral significance of change in the ownership of the acquired firm. There is little empirical evidence in this regard—this study provides a

[16] Documentation of this point is difficult. There is no study of the extent to which entry to new markets by large corporations has involved corporate acquisition of one sort or another. On the other hand, the extent of merger activity on the part of large corporations generally would rather clearly suggest that this is indeed true. See Ralph L. Nelson, *Merger Movements in American Industry, 1895-1956* (Princeton: Princeton University Press, 1959), and also *Economic Report on Corporate Mergers, op.cit.*, pp. 29-67.

[17] The following argument also appears in Charles H. Berry, "Economic Policy and the Conglomerate Merger," *St. John's Law Review*, Vol. 44, Special Edition, Spring 1970, pp. 266-281. For related comments, see Martin L. Lindahl, "Conglomerate Mergers and Acquisitions: An Introduction," and William G. Shepherd, "The Conglomerate Merger Wave: An Introduction," *St. John's Law Review, op.cit.*, pp. 37-41 and 45-48, respectively.

thread—but the issue is clearly central to the evaluation not only of conglomerate (diversifying) mergers, but indeed of all mergers.

Large-Scale Acquisitions

For example, consider large acquisitions. The merger of two corporations, each large and each dominant within its industry, and each showing no sign of present or impending financial distress, would appear, without further qualification, to accomplish little in terms of structural change that could be considered *a priori* desirable. If the two (or more) industries involved are *totally* independent, any resulting economy or social advantage would have to be attributed to the superior managerial competence of the acquiring firm, which is not only difficult if not impossible to determine, but also is a rather unsatisfactory basis upon which to build a case for the merger of two large organizations.[18] This is especially true if other adverse consequences might be present.

Where, however, the markets are not independent, but linked either vertically or horizontally, or where there is a technological overlap in the production process, or where common marketing or information facilities might be employed, there *is* the possibility that the combination might generate increased efficiency and the resulting social gain. But there is also the possibility that such a merger would carry with it a likelihood that real or potential competition between the merging firms would be eliminated. If each firm is large, and if an economy of joint operation in both (or all) markets *is* present, each firm, in the absence of merger, is a prime candidate for entry to the market of the other. It is precisely this possibility of increased efficiency that creates the possibility

[18] Bork, nevertheless, does. See Robert Bork, *loc.cit.*

that competition would be lessened by such a merger. Indeed, to carry the argument to its extreme, the desire of two such large firms to merge might well be taken as an indication that an economy of joint operation is present, and one result of such a merger would be the elimination of entry that might otherwise have occurred. This is true even if the "economy" of joint operation is little more than gratification of the desire of corporate managers for growth for growth's sake.

Hence in both cases—either where markets are unrelated, or when some interrelationship is present—the merger of large and dominant firms has little to recommend it. The exception would occur when one party to the merger is failing. In that event, however, the failing corporation would not likely be dominant, and the merger itself would be as much a liquidation as an acquisition.[19]

Small-Scale Acquisitions

Where, however, one of the merging firms is small, the situation is not the same. For the smaller firm, access to the retained earnings, or the borrowing capacity, of the large firm may provide the counterpart to needed investment funds at rates favorable to those obtainable else-

---

[19] Large firms *do*, on occasion, fail, and the consequences are not always sensibly interpreted. The Federal Trade Commission, for example, in examining turnover among the 1,000 largest manufacturing corporations, distinguishes between "liquidation" and "acquisition" (and also relative decline in size). The implication is that firms such as Packard, Nash, and Studebaker, to name a few well-known examples, would, in the absence of their acquisition (or partial acquisition) have remained viable, independent competitors in (presumably) the automotive field. See *Economic Report on Corporate Mergers, op.cit.*, pp. 713-714.

where.[20] In addition, or alternatively, the merger may establish for the product(s) of the smaller firm access to national markets and merchandising—perhaps even the acquisition of a nationally known corporate name—at costs less than those which would be incurred by a replication of the facilities of the large firm even were that feasible.[21] Similar savings might be present if further development in the industry of the smaller firm required a technological base that could be incorporated into the operations of the larger firm.[22] For any number of such reasons, the merger might provide *real* economies for the small firm, and those would be more likely the greater the opportunities for growth within the industry of the small firm.

Such an industry is likely to be a candidate—and the results of Chapter VI are an attempt to detect it—for the entry of large nationally active corporations. The acquisition of a small firm, in an industry offering an opportunity for the further exploitation of current corporate

[20] See S. H. Archer and L. G. Faerber, "Size of Firm and the Cost of Externally Acquired Equity Capital," *Journal of Finance*, Vol. 21, March 1966, pp. 69-83.

[21] In a sense, the argument is that there are externalities of ownership. See Francis Bator, "The Anatomy of Market Failure," in William Breit and Harold Hochman (eds.), *Readings in Microeconomics* (New York: Holt, Rinehart & Winston, 1968), pp. 457-476, esp. pp. 465-476.

[22] This argument is made most clearly by Richard R. Nelson in "The Simple Economics of Basic Scientific Research," *Journal of Political Economy*, Vol. 67, June 1959, pp. 297-306. See also Edwin S. Mansfield, "Size of Firm, Market Structure and Innovation," *Journal of Political Economy*, Vol. 71, December 1963, pp. 556-576 and "Industrial Research and Development Expenditures: Determinants, Prospects, and Relation to Size of Firm," *Journal of Political Economy*, Vol. 72, August 1964, pp. 319-340.

facilities, can be a relatively inexpensive means of obtaining institutional knowledge and some of the managerial skills that would be required even for entry *de novo*.[23] The merger may be a means of minimizing the costs of facilities that would be required in any case. No new firm is added by the merger, but if, as may frequently be the case, there are economies created by the merger, the acquired firm—which by assumption is here small— should, as a consequence of its change in ownership, be in an improved competitive position within its market.

Just as previously, where potential competition between the merging firms has been eliminated, but where the acquired firm is *small within* its market, it would be difficult to argue that a substantial lessening of competition is the result.[24] The converse is more likely. At the very most, the change is negligible. Expected economies from joint operation do not materialize. Both (or all) markets behave pretty much as they would have otherwise. The industries are independent in the sense outlined earlier. Entry by the large corporation to the market of the smaller has been facilitated to the extent that the merger was less expensive to the acquiring firm than the corresponding cost of equivalent entry *de novo*.[25] Some corporate growth by merger has occurred.

[23] See Jesse W. Markham, "Survey of the Evidence and Findings on Mergers," in National Bureau of Economic Research, *Business Concentration and Price Policy* (Princeton: Princeton University Press, 1955), pp. 141-212, esp. pp. 174-180.

[24] For a different interpretation, see *Economic Report on Corporate Mergers, op.cit.*, pp. 220-225.

[25] This implies that such a merger can be considered essentially the equivalent of entry *de novo*. If the merger *is* entry, and if such entry *is* desirable, it follows rather obviously that such mergers are desirable.

Anti-Merger Law

Curiously enough, this suggests that the contemporary interpretation of merger law with respect to horizontal and vertical mergers is readily and appropriately extended to the conglomerate merger. For example, where two corporations with products actively competing in the same (horizontal) market merge, the effect is obviously and immediately the removal of a competitor from that market. If neither firm is failing—as would be likely in the presence of scale economies within that market—a lessening of competition can reasonably be inferred.[26] The potential damage from the prohibition of such mergers is chiefly that the development of a larger, more efficient firm is delayed and restricted to the outcome of such competitive pressure as may exist within that market. The danger of permitting the merger is the development, unjustified by economic considerations, of a market structure conducive to patterns of oligopoly behavior. That danger is clearly greater the more concentrated the industry to begin with, and the larger the size, relative to that market, of the firms proposing to merge.[27] Within that framework, a judgment regarding the probability of a substantial lessening of competition can be made. It has been made restrictively in recent years.[28]

With vertical mergers the situation is not vastly different. Where neither market is highly concentrated, and

[26] And in general has. See A. D. Neale, *The Antitrust Laws of the United States* (Cambridge: Cambridge University Press, 1966), pp. 178-202.

[27] See James S. Campbell and William G. Shepherd, "Leading Firm Conglomerate Mergers," *Antitrust Bulletin*, Vol. 12, Winter 1968, pp. 1,361-1,382.

[28] *Ibid.*, esp. pp. 191-197.

where the merging firms are each small within their respective market, the probability of a substantial lessening of competition as a consequence of the merger is low. Where, however, the merging firms are large—and the concept of size is obviously a subjective one—the courts have generally regarded the merger as likely to "foreclose," or as being capable of foreclosing, a substantial share of the market for the indeterminate good in question.[29] The cost to such a policy is that production and distribution economies that *may* be implicit in the denied vertical integration are thereby lost or delayed. The realization of such economies may not be by merger where market shares are substantial, but only by internal growth or by the acquisition of a market share that does not pose the possibility of substantial foreclosure.

The danger from freely permitting such mergers—the primary danger—is that the potential competition between the parties to the merger is eliminated in the event of the merger, *and that where those firms are large there is a reasonable likelihood either that entry would occur or that the threat of such entry is a significant regulatory force by itself.*

For example, if economies of joint (vertical) operation are present, it is likely that each of the two firms, if their merger were denied, would integrate backwards and forwards, respectively, to gain the benefit of such economies. Each firm is presumably a more likely entrant to the market of the other than any other firm of equivalent size that is active in neither market. Alternatively, and perhaps even more important, if structure at either stage of the vertical process is conducive to non-competitive

[29] See, for example, F. M. Scherer, *Industrial Market Structure and Economic Performance* (Chicago: Rand McNally, 1970), pp. 462-463.

behavior at that stage, that too creates an incentive for entry by those corporations active at the other stage where the costs of that non-competitive behavior are borne directly.[30] Merger, under those circumstances, would permit an accommodation between potentially competitive firms that would preserve the opportunity for the continued exploitation of existing market imperfection. If such mergers are proscribed, as they have been (though for somewhat different reasons), such accommodation is denied.

In this sense, the public policy of vertical mergers is closely analogous to that of horizontal mergers. The distinction lies only in that the competition is actual in one instance, and potential in the other. But the competition itself is horizontal in each instance.

The case of the conglomerate merger is one step removed, but the analytic framework can and should be identical. With conglomerate mergers, the link between the markets of the firms proposing to merge is less clear than when the merger is vertical. The potential expansion of one corporation to the market of the other is correspondingly less certain. The cost in terms of lost potential (or actual) competition associated with the consummation of such mergers is less obvious. But it can be present, and indeed will be present increasingly to the extent that there are economic advantages to combining productive activity in different markets within the framework of a single corporate entity.

The public policy of the conglomerate merger ought therefore to be directly related to the public policy of the vertical merger. In both cases the merger is between corporations that are potential, not active, competitors. In both cases the merger will foreclose the entry that

[30] *Ibid.*, pp. 87-88.

167

might have brought the merging firms into direct intra-market (horizontal) competition. In both cases, where the merging corporations are large, and where there are potential gains from joint operation present, there is reason to believe that in the absence of merger entry is reasonably probable.[31] This is perhaps less so in the case of the conglomerate merger where the relationship between the markets involved is less clear. Nevertheless, such interrelationship *can* be present. That kind of interrelationship is one of the few convincing elementary lessons of micro-economic theory.

Merger "Rules"

This being the case, the policy notion ought to be that no firm capable of independent entry—and that means a large firm—should be permitted to acquire by merger a significant proportion of any market in which, prior to the merger, that firm could reasonably be expected to be a potential competitor. If one believes that the regulatory agencies have the judgment and the facilities necessary to identify and sustain the presence of market relationships indicating potential entry and competition, this in turn suggests a rule of quantitative substantiality with respect to conglomerate mergers along much the same lines as those currently employed in vertical mergers, and currently argued in conglomerate mergers.[32] If, however, those facilities and that judgment are suspect, the alternative is a merger rule prohibiting the acquisition by any large firm of a leading market position in *any* industry. In either case, the objective should be to seek to retain

[31] See James S. Campbell and William G. Shepherd, *loc.cit.*, and also *Task Force Report on Antitrust Policy, op.cit.*, pp. iii-1 to iii-13.

[32] *Ibid.*

wherever possible the benefits of the large firm as a potential (or actual) entrant, while avoiding those attributes of the conglomerate merger that may augment or perpetuate existing market power.

In either case as well, there is a real danger that corporate size, market position, or for that matter industries or markets, may be defined so narrowly as to lose much of the power of the potential competition of the large corporation. One proposed merger rule would, for example, block the merger of two firms, each in a different industry, and each with sales of little more than $10 million.[33] The proposed conglomerate merger rule of the Neale Task Force Report on Antitrust Policy, which is more lenient, would nevertheless define an industry within which a large firm might not acquire any of the leading four producers as ". . . a relevant economic market (with sales of at least $10 million), *appropriately* defined with reference to geographical area (which may be the United States or another geographic area) and product or service. . . ."[34] Discretion does not end with the introduction of such a rule. As is frequent in the analysis of public policy toward business, the principle is more easily stated than applied.

One finding of this study is that, without such rules entry by 461 large firms, taken as a whole, was associated with decreasing concentration in concentrated industries. It is that potential which any such merger rule ought to preserve rather than destroy. A second is evidence that, in those concentrated industries, entry by small corporations will not do the job.

---

[33] James S. Campbell and William G. Shepherd, *op.cit.*, pp. 1,363-1,364.

[34] *Task Force Report on Antitrust Policy*, *op.cit.*, pp. B-3 and B-4, emphasis added.

A COMMENT

What is reported here pushes limited data to an extreme that automatically questions the validity of any finding. Had this work been based on confidential Census records, nothing other than some appendix tables (which could be readily omitted) contained herein would be disclosure. There is no reason that work of this sort ought to be forced to rely on the type of data employed here. Far more precise measures of entry, penetration, and structure could still be employed without impinging on disclosure rules even as they now exist. The findings would not only be more reliable; they might be far more interesting. They would be more interesting still if the products of foreign manufacture imported and sold in this country could be merged—as they should be—with these Census records of the performance of domestic industry. Trade is one of the most powerful, and least used, weapons of antitrust action. That its impact on the structure of domestic markets is hidden in the available measures of market structure is little short of scandalous.

It is not clear, however, that these Census disclosure rules have any valid applicability to the large industrial corporation. Much corporate law to the contrary, the large industrial corporation is not an individual with the rights of an individual. Two hundred corporations account for almost half of all domestic value added in manufacture. That is not necessarily bad—but it may be—and it would be nice to know. To know, however, requires information that is at present assembled and concealed by the same public agency. The large corporation exists as a consequence of public policy in the form of enabling legislation. It is not inappropriate that records permitting

170

an evaluation of that policy be made publicly available. For example, the following:

(1) For all corporations with consolidated domestic assets of some stated amount—say $250 million—disclosure for each corporation, in each Census year, the total value of shipments by that corporation's establishments classified by 5-digit product class.

(2) For each such corporation, disclosure in each Census year, the total value of shipments *internal to the firm* by establishments of that corporation, again classified by 5-digit product class.

(3) For each such corporation, disclosure in each Census year of the value added, the value of shipments, the employment and the payroll of the establishments of that corporation, classified by 4-digit industry.

In each instance, this information could be assembled from Census reports for individual establishments. With the exception of (2) this information is currently assembled by the Bureau of the Census but is not available to non-Census analysts. It should be but it will not be unless attitudes toward the rights to confidentiality of major corporations are markedly re-defined.

At present, the Federal Trade Commission is actively pressing, though not terribly successfully, for the establishment of an "Annual Line of Business Report Program" as part of the Commission's Quarterly Financial Statistical Program.[35] The line of Business Reports would contain, as proposed, estimates of the profitability for large corporations of several hundred product lines defined for this purpose by the Commission. Those estimates would

[35] Federal Trade Commission, Bureau of Economics Staff, Statement of Purpose, Annual Line of Business Report Program (mimeographed, 1973).

171

be prepared within the Commission from information relating to sales and costs reported by large corporations for their establishments. The purpose of this proposal is the dissemination of profit rates by product lines—of interest, presumably, to the competitors and potential competitors of these large firms—not the development of data that would disclose (outside the Commission) shifts in the relative market positions of leading and large firms. For that purpose, what is needed is public disclosure of the product line sales of *individual* large corporations—data of the sort that are here *estimated* for the *Fortune* corporations. That would not (though it could) be a product of the F.T.C. product line proposal which explicitly states that *"names and data for individual firms will not be made public."*[36] The implication is either that analysis of the sort here called for (including, for example, assessment of the success of information generating function of the line of Business Reports) would not be done, or that it would be done only internally by the Commission and at the initiative of the Commission. Neither arrangement would be apt to be optimal. If the full structural impact of large scale corporate diversification is to be adequately understood, and if the public policy of related corporate control is to be intelligently formulated, data that link the large corporation to its markets must be in the public domain.

[36] *Ibid.*, p. 1, emphasis added.

Index

census records, *see* U.S. Bureau
of the Census
city products, 53
Clayton Act, *1950* amendment
of, 4
Collins, Norman R., 9n
Comanor, William S., 17n
Commonwealth Oil, 52, 53,
56-57
competition: antitrust stat-
tutes worded in terms of,
3n; conventional economic
theory of, 17; cross-sub-
sidization and, 20-22; effect
of diversification on, 38,
157-59; effect of horizontal
mergers on, 165-69; effect
of large-scale acquisition on,
161-62; effect of small-scale
acquisition on, 162-64; effect
of vertical mergers on,
165-69; exclusive dealing
and, 24-25; multi-product
firms and, 19-30; non-price
concessions and, 25, 26, 27;
reciprocal dealing and, 26-
30; single-product firm and,
19
concentration: as common
measure of market struc-
ture, 132; data available on,
124; and ease of entry and
exit, 126; effect of entry by
larger firms on, 122-23,
129-44, 157, 159, 169;
effect of merger on, 165-69;
effect of weighted figures
on, 18n, 34; and entry barriers, 35-38, 135-44 *passim*;
gauge of, 17; and model of

structural change, 132-36,
140; ratio of, 17, 127, 132;
recent changes in, 5, 16, 18n,
30, 33-35. *See also 8*-firm
concentration; *4*-firm concentration
*Concentration Ratios in Manu-
facturing Industry, 1967,*
137n
conglomerate: and expansion
to monopoly, 158; leverage
of, 19-30; mergers of, 30n,
158n, 161, 165-69; pro-
posed rule on, 168-69; and
reciprocal dealing, 28n
corporate acquisition: distin-
guished from liquidation,
162; economies involved in,
161, 163, 164; effects of on
market structure, 48, 49,
161-62, 164, 165-69; as
means of entry to new markets, 48-51, 160; and tendency to stay within same
2-digit industry group, 37n;
and *33* "merged" corporations, 47, 57-58. *See also*
horizontal acquisition; merger; vertical integration
corporate earnings: defined,
68; and rate of entry and
exit, 125-26; related to corporate growth, 67, 69, 102,
104-106, 123, 129, 155
corporate growth: commonly
held opinions on, 153; defined, 67; entry as best explanatory variable of, 74,
155; of largest industrials,
4, 9-16, 30n, 106, 153n;

179

ownership, of corporation, 8-9

Packard, 162n
Parke-Davis, 3
Pechman, Joseph A., vii
PEN, 134, 136-37, 145
Penrose, Edith T., 97n
Penrose-type hypothesis, 97n,
101-102
percent change, 69
PEXT, 145
Plant and Product Directory,
vi, 48n, 60n, 94n: advan-
tages of data from, 40; data
available in, 52-54, 55; data
from compared to Census
data, 39-40; and data on
208 4-digit industries, 124-
25, 137, 145-52; limitations
of data from, vi, 40, 49,
53-54, 124, 137n, 145-46;
sources used in compilation
of, 53-54
plant facilities: capital requirements for, 36n; designation
of, 54; entry and exit of,
41-47; of *494-461* large industrials, 40-46; of *460* large
industrials, 60; location of as
growth factor, 70; of *33*
"merged" corporations, 48-
51, 55-56; turnover of, 40-
47; weighting of, 66n, 76-78,
127n
Preston, Lee E., 17n, 108n
price: concessions in, 25, 26,
27, 28; controls on, 22n,
23n; conventional economic
theory on, 16, 25; cross-
subsidization and, 20-22;

discrimination in, 22, 23n;
and exclusive dealing, 24-25;
reciprocal dealing and, 26-
30; rigidity of, 20, 26; tying
contracts and, 22-23
primary product specialization
ratio, 128n
production: determined by
employment figures, 54, 66n,
76-77; weighting relative importance of, 66. *See also*
products
products: data on, 39; effect of
entry and exit on, 71, 74,
91-95; effect of merger on,
49; increase in number reported by *460* large industrials, 60-62, 73, 155;
increase in without diversification, 64-66, 73, 155; ship-
ment of used as variable in
measuring entry and exit,
126-28, 132, 136-37;
weighting of, 54, 66n, 77
profit measures, 128
PROGRO, 99
projected growth, 68-69
public policy: on disclosure of
data, 39, 170-72; goals of,
6n, 167-68; influences on,
3-5; and measure of corporate size, 3n; on merger,
3-5, 165-69

Quandt, R. E., 128n
*Quarterly Financial Report for
Manufacturing Corpora-
tions*, 9, 11-12
Quarterly Financial Statistical
Program, 171-72

reciprocal dealing: and conglomerate acquisition, 28n; defined, 19; effect of, 26-30; and link with multiple pricing, 25-26
Revere, Paul, 14
Rose, Sanford, 30n, 31
Rubinstein, Joel, viii

Sadowsky, George, viii
scale economy, *see* economy of scale
Scherer, F. M.: 4-digit industries used by, 124n; on market concentration, 18n, 34n, 36n; on mergers, 166n; on oligopoly, 20n
Schlumberger, 47n
Schmalensee, Richard, 26n
Scitovsky, Tibor, 35n
Seaboard Finance, 14
Securities Exchange Commission (SEC), 9, 16
Shepherd, William G., 18n, 113n, 124n; on diversification and market power, 131, 134, 135, 153n, 160n, 165n, 168n, 169n; on need for further data, 142-43; and use of coverage ratio, 127n
single-product firm, and competition, 19
Smallwood, Dennis, viii
specialization, 73, 77, 128n
Standard and Poor's establishment tapes, 53
Standard Fashion Co., 25
Standard Industrial Classification (SIC), 52, 56, 71: measures of diversification

based on, 156; problems associated with, 73, 107-108, 156, 159; revision of, 124; suggested vertical reclassification of, 108n
steel industry, 70
Stigler, George J., 5n, 28n, 129n
Studebaker, 162n
Studies by the Staff of the Cabinet Committee on Price Stability: on change in structure of 4-digit industries, 17n, 33n; on diversification of largest corporations, 153n
study: advantages of data used in, 40; Census data compared to Fortune data used, 39, 40, 53, 54; data on mergers, 55-57, 137n; data on *208* 4-digit industries, 124-25, 137, 145-52; data sources for *494-461* large industrials, 39-40, 52-56, 124-25; data sources for *460* large industrials, 59-60, 76-78; limitations of data available for, 40, 49, 53-54, 73, 106-108, 124, 137n, 145-46, 156, 159; period of, 6, 40, 124, 129, 154; preparation of data file for, 55-56; questions asked by, 153; three-part analysis of, 38-39
subsidiaries, and problems of growth measurement, 8-16 *passim*
Sunbeam, 3

Library of Congress Cataloging in Publication Data
Berry, Charles Harris, 1930-
    Corporate growth and diversification.

    Includes bibliographical references and index.
    1. Conglomerate corporations—United States—
Addresses, essays, lectures.   I. Title.
HD2756.U5B46 1974   338.8′3   74-2960
ISBN 0-691-04202-0